essential
FONDUE
COOKBOOK

**75 DECADENT RECIPES TO
DELIGHT & ENTERTAIN**

essential
FONDUE
COOKBOOK

—

ERIN HARRIS

Photography by Iain Bagwell

callisto
publishing
an imprint of Sourcebooks

Interior and Cover Designer: Michael Patti
Art Producer: Sara Feinstein
Editor: Mo Mozuch
Production Editor: Rachel Taenzler
Photography © Iain Bagwell. Food styling by Loren Wood.

Published by Callisto Publishing LLC C/O Sourcebooks LLC
P.O. Box 4410, Naperville, Illinois 60567-4410
(630) 961-3900
callistopublishing.com

Printed and bound in China
OGP 2

This cookbook is dedicated to my family, who raised me to appreciate cheese in its many forms and supported my culinary journey from the very beginning. This life would not be nearly as delicious without you!

contents

Introduction *xi*

1 How Do You Fondue? *1*

2 How to Make It Fun-Due *11*

3 Cheese Fondue *23*

Traditional Swiss Fondue *26*

Moitié-Moitié Fondue *28*

French Fondue *29*

Italian Fonduta *30*

Spanish Fondue *31*

Truffle Fondue *33*

Hot Queso Fondue *34*

Indian Masala Fondue *36*

Basil Pesto Fondue *38*

French Onion Fondue *40*

Baked Brie Fondue *42*

Canadian Maple-Bacon Fondue *43*

American Cheeseburger Fondue *44*

Cheddar and Ale Fondue *46*

Blue Cheese and Leek Fondue *47*

Pimento Cheese Fondue *48*

Fondue in a Pumpkin *50*

Cacio e Pepe Fondue *52*

Spinach and Artichoke Fondue *53*

Wild Mushroom and Herb Fondue *55*

Jalapeño Popper Fondue *57*

4 **Fondue Bourguignonne** 61

Classic Bourguignonne
Hot Oil Fondue 63

Bagna Cauda Fondue 64

Asian Tempura Fondue 66

Spanish-Style Oil
Fondue 68

Italian-Style Oil Fondue 70

German-Style Oil Fondue 72

Greek-Style Oil Fondue 74

5 **Fondue Hot Pot** 77

Classic Beef Broth Hot Pot 79

Classic Chicken Broth Hot Pot 80

Miso and Lemongrass Broth 81

Coq Au Vin Fondue 83

Mushroom Broth Fondue 85

Tomato-Saffron Broth Fondue 87

French Onion Broth Fondue 89

Spicy Szechuan Hot Pot 91

Spicy Mexican Broth Fondue 93

Greek Lemon and Garlic Broth
Fondue 95

6 Dessert Fondue 99

Caramel Apple–Brie Fondue 101
Spiked English Custard Fondue 103
Salted Caramel Fondue 105
Chocolate Peanut Butter Fondue 107
Chocolate Crème Fraîche Fondue 108
Chocolate-Espresso Fondue 109
Bourbon-Butterscotch Fondue 110
Cheesecake Fondue 111
White Chocolate–
Marshmallow Fondue 112
Maple Cream Fondue 113
Vegan Toasted Coconut Fondue 114
Bananas Foster Fondue 115

7 Dippers & Sauces 119

Steak Sauce 120
Béarnaise Sauce 122
Peanut Sauce 124
Tartar Sauce 125
Mayonnaise 126
Curry Aioli 128
Horseradish Cream 129
Roquefort Dip 130
Vietnamese Nuoc Cham Sauce 131
Tzatziki Sauce 132
Rouille Sauce 133
Korean Gochujang Ketchup 134

Classic Beef Broth *135*

Chicken Broth *137*

Grilled Vegetables *138*

Steamed Vegetables *140*

Tempura Batter *142*

Scottish Shortbread Cookies *143*

Angel Food Cake *145*

Half-Pound Cake *147*

Almond Biscotti *149*

Crostini *151*

Gougères *152*

Crisp Gingersnap Cookies *154*

Garlic Bread Knots *156*

Measurement Conversions *158*

Index *160*

INTRODUCTION

My culinary adventure started when I was very young, as my mom's helper in the kitchen. I recall rolling out scraps of pie dough to make smaller versions of whatever pie she was baking and grating cheese for pots of her Cheddar cheese fondue—a family favorite.

My first real job in the kitchen was as a prep cook in a local bistro. I peeled garlic and chopped herbs for hours on end, a memory punctuated by the aromas that lingered on my fingers afterward. I went on to complete a diploma in culinary arts and achieve a Red Seal chef certificate, a nationally recognized examination on the art of traditional French cookery.

My love of cooking deepened as I dove into a second diploma for Italian cuisine, which took me on an adventure to Italy where my love of cheese took hold. As a young culinary student, my travels continued to France and Switzerland, where cheese fondue is a way of life. Today, I enjoy hosting fondue parties for my friends and family—an excuse to get together and break bread around pots of melty cheese and chocolate. I hope that this book takes you on your own fondue journey. It's a delicious way to experience all of life's flavors.

1

how do you fondue?

IN THIS chapter, we explore the art of hosting a fondue party and the history of fondue, including how Swiss cheese fondue became celebrated all over the world. It also explains how to choose the right fondue pot for whatever style you're serving. Keeping a well-stocked pantry is vital. Use the list provided to outfit your pantry with the essential ingredients required to make fondue any night of the week. You'll also learn how to choose the right cheese for your fondue, giving you the confidence to make suitable substitutions.

WHAT IS FONDUE?

The simplest explanation is that fondue is a sweet or savory hot dish served in a communal pot with long-handled forks, with a selection of accompanying dippers and sauces. The French word *fondre* means "to melt," and cheese fondue was first documented in the early 1700s in France as nothing more than warmed wine mixed with melted cheese and served with bread for dipping. The addition of cornstarch modernized fondue in the early 1900s in Switzerland, producing the smooth, emulsified cheese fondue we know today.

After World War II, the Swiss Cheese Union promoted cheese fondue internationally to increase the consumption of Swiss-made cheese and to bolster the Swiss economy. This effort succeeded, resulting in cheese fondue being named as the national dish of Switzerland. Fondue didn't become popular in North America until the 1960s, when an appearance at the World's Fair put it on the menu at some chic new restaurants. Household use of fuel-warmed chafing dishes soon became the norm, and fondue pots were common wedding gifts for the modern host. At one point, the Swiss government reportedly spent more money subsidizing dairy farms than it did on their military!

Although Swiss cheese fondue is perhaps the most internationally well-known style of fondue, this book also features versions of fondue found in cultures around the world. Hot oil fondue is an alternative to cheese fondue and is known in France and Switzerland as fondue Bourguignonne. You cook tender cuts of meats and vegetables in a communal fondue pot full of hot oil. Fondue Bourguignonne's highlight is the array of sauces that turn an otherwise simple dish into a gourmet experience, including traditional French condiments like homemade mayonnaise, Béarnaise sauce, and garlic aioli. Today's fusion cuisine also adds possibilities from Thai-inspired peanut sauce to curry aioli and blue cheese dip. The Piedmont region of Northern Italy is home to *bagna cauda*—a warmed bath of olive oil, garlic, and anchovies served at a much lower temperature than fondue Bourguignonne and offered as a communal dish for dipping fresh vegetables, grilled meats, and Italian breads.

A style of fondue that requires a bubbling pot of boldly flavored broth to cook meats, seafood, and vegetables is found throughout Asia. In China it is known as Hot Pot, and in Japan it's called Shabu Shabu. Serve your chosen variety with a bowl of noodles or steamed rice for slurping up the delicious broth. Fondue can be a heavy meal, so cooking with broth offers a lighter option that doesn't sacrifice flavor.

Switzerland offers more than just exceptionally delicious cheese; it's also home to some of the best chocolate found anywhere in the world. It was only a matter of time, then, until high-quality chocolate would be melted and served as a dessert fondue, with fresh fruit and cubes of cake and pastries. In this book, you will find an array of dessert fondue recipes that combine all our favorite flavors, like New Orleans-inspired Bananas Foster Fondue (page 115), Bourbon-Butterscotch Fondue (page 110) (that coincidentally makes an amazing sundae topping), and Chocolate-Espresso Fondue (page 109)—the ultimate dessert for the chocolate and coffee lover in your life.

No matter the style of fondue you choose to prepare, one thing always remains the same: the company. Fondue is a timeless experience for you and your guests to enjoy together, sharing an atmosphere of coziness and warmth around the table.

GONE TO POT

Choosing the right fondue pot is an important first step. There is nothing more frustrating than going to all the effort of preparing a fondue feast only to scorch it, or worse, end up with a cracked fondue pot that couldn't withstand the higher heat of hot oil or broth-style fondue. The following list will help you choose a pot and offers tips to confidently host a successful fondue party from start to finish. If you already have a fondue pot, take some time to read the manufacturer's instructions so you know what it can and cannot do.

Electric Fondue Pots

Electric fondue pots have gained popularity in recent years for good reason. This style is a versatile option for serving all types of fondue. They typically come with a stainless steel or cast-iron insert that can withstand high heat for broth- and oil-based fondue and a ceramic insert for cheese and dessert fondue. They also feature a handy temperature control, so you can set the temperature very low for cheese and dessert fondue without fear of scorching the bottom. There are only a couple of minor things to consider when purchasing an electric fondue pot. First, decide on your desired cord length. You'll have to keep the pot plugged in, so you'll either need to set it up close to an outlet or have an extension cord handy. Typically, electric fondue pots are meant to keep things warm, not cook them, so most pots are not designed for stovetop use. You'll likely be preparing your fondue on the stovetop first, then transferring it to the fondue pot.

Enameled Cast-Iron Fondue Pots

An enameled cast-iron fondue pot is the authentic and traditional vessel for serving cheese fondue. These pots are heavy and durable, and the enamel coating makes them easy to clean—a nice feature if you have ever had to scrub cheese off the bottom of a scorched pot. This style of fondue pot comes with an open flame–style burner that sits underneath the pot and requires liquid Sterno or another ethanol-based gel fuel to burn. These pots go from stove to table, and the small burners aren't strong enough to properly heat oil- or broth-based fondue for very long. They can be an option for dessert fondue, although the pot is typically too large for the smaller serving size of this fondue variety. Aesthetically, this style of fondue pot will look the part on your table, adding to the cozy atmosphere of a traditional Swiss cheese fondue party.

Stainless Steel and Aluminum Fondue Pots

Stainless steel and aluminum fondue pots are ideal for serving hot oil and broth-style fondue, like fondue Bourguignonne and Hot Pot. They are thin and lightweight and require very little time to heat up, so your meat and vegetables will be properly cooked through. These pots are not recommended for cheese and dessert fondue unless they come with a ceramic insert. The thin bottom of the stainless steel and aluminum pot will scorch the cheese and dessert fondue quickly, making your meal a challenge to enjoy and a big mess to clean up. This style of fondue pot often comes with a splash guard that sits on the top of the pot and will help eliminate splatters on your table—and your guests—from the hot oil and broth.

Glazed Ceramic Fondue Pots

Glazed ceramic fondue pots are available in several different sizes and are a suitable option for both cheese and dessert fondue. Larger ceramic vessels often come equipped with an open-flame burner similar to an enameled cast-iron pot, whereas smaller sets typically include a tealight candle as the heat source, which produces much less heat. Thus, the latter is ideal for keeping dessert fondue warm but not too hot. Glazed ceramic cannot withstand the high heat necessary for hot oil and broth-style fondue and may crack or break. If you only plan to serve cheese or dessert fondue and your space is limited, consider a smaller glazed ceramic fondue pot.

A FONDUE PANTRY

A well-stocked pantry makes it easy to serve fondue on a whim. Since most of the recipes in this book come together in less than 30 minutes, fondue is a viable meal option for any night of the week. Use this list to keep a selection of fondue pantry essentials on hand.

Brandy. This spirit is used to add a sharp and heady bite to both sweet and savory fondue.

Broth, chicken and beef. Since there are very few ingredients used in fondue, the flavor and quality of your broth makes a difference. Choose higher-quality, ready-made broth over bouillon cubes, or use our recipe for Classic Beef Broth (page 135) and Chicken Broth (page 137).

Cooking oil. Peanut, sunflower seed, or safflower seed oil are neutral in flavor and have high smoke points, perfect for frying.

Cornstarch. Cornstarch produces a smooth, emulsified cheese fondue and is the main thickening agent used in this cookbook.

Dijon mustard. This is an all-around good mustard to have on hand for emulsifying sauces, adding a spicy bite and well-rounded flavor to almost any cheese dish or sauce.

Dry white wine. Although most cheese fondue recipes can be made without wine, it is still the preferred liquid because it adds flavor and helps emulsify the cheese.

Evaporated milk. You can use evaporated milk instead of heavy cream in a pinch. It will add a creamy consistency to your caramel sauce, dessert custard, or cheese fondue.

Garlic. This herb is a flavor booster for broth, cheese fondue, and sauces.

Mayonnaise. Mayonnaise is a foundation for many of the sauce recipes listed in this book. Make your own on page 126.

Onions. Caramelize them for French Onion Broth (page 89) and French Onion Fondue (page 40), or add them to any broth for extra flavor.

Peanut butter. Peanut dipping sauce can be made in five minutes and adds flavor and intrigue to your fondue experience. It goes great with chocolate, too.

Semisweet chocolate. Chocolate comes in many different levels of quality. I recommend buying the best quality for your budget and letting the flavors of your chocolate shine through.

Sugar. Sugar is the most important ingredient for making homemade caramel and adding sweetness to your dessert fondue.

Worcestershire sauce. Worcestershire is a savory sauce that adds depth and richness to Cheddar fondue recipes.

TO WINE OR NOT TO WINE?

Fondue is traditionally made with an emulsion of wine or beer and cheese. The tartaric acid in wine helps the cheese emulsify into the liquid, which produces a more luxurious cheese fondue. This mixture produces a delightful taste, but it's not for everyone. If you prefer to keep the alcohol out of your fondue, you can easily substitute the same amount of good-quality vegetable or chicken broth. If you eliminate wine from your fondue, make sure to thicken the liquid with cornstarch before adding your cheese to ensure a proper emulsification. The broth will add some extra flavor, so choose one that will match well with the other fondue components.

2

how to make it fun-due

FONDUE IS so much more than the pot it's served in. It's a communal way of eating that unites different cultures and flavors, and it offers countless ways to indulge. If you celebrate Chinese New Year, Spicy Szechuan Hot Pot (page 91) is the perfect dish since this holiday is observed during the colder winter months. Celebrating a birthday with a Cheesecake Fondue (page 111) is a great way to make the guest of honor feel special. If you host game day parties, Pimento Cheese Fondue (page 48) makes a great tailgating dish. Serve French Onion Fondue (page 40) during the holidays to add a warm and festive spirit you and your guests will enjoy.

SETTING THE TABLE

Fondue can be a relaxing way to enjoy a social meal, but it can get crowded and messy if you don't set a proper table. The following list of items will help you figure out what you need to optimize your seating and serving arrangements.

Dipping basket. This is a small metal basket great for cooking veggies and noodles in hot broth fondue.

Extra fuel and a lighter. If you are using a fondue pot with an open-flame heat source, have extra fuel and a lighter nearby. If you run out of fuel, your fondue will turn cold very quickly.

Fondue pot. Also known as a *caquelon*, this pot is the star of the show and will keep your fondue warm until the pot is empty.

Long-handled forks. Each guest should have their own long-handled fondue fork for dipping into the fondue pot. Find a set that's color-coded so guests can keep track of their forks in the pot.

Paper towels. When serving hot oil fondue, place a few layers of paper towels on a plate near the pot for draining fried foods as they cool.

Plates. Each guest should receive their own plate at their place setting for building a plate of dippers and resting their fondue forks between dipping. Invest in raclette plates featuring divided sections if you plan to make fondue a regular thing.

Ramekins. Offer a selection of two or three sauces in ramekins with a small spoon.

Shot glasses. Heavy cheese and hot oil fondue are traditionally served with an intermission shot of Kirschwasser or another spirit of your choice to help you digest.

Tablecloth and napkins. Fondue can be a messy affair, so it is wise to protect your table from spills and splatters with a tablecloth. Offer your guests their own napkins and have a few extra close by, just in case.

Thermometer. If you are serving hot oil or broth-style fondue and you are cooking meats and seafood, it is wise to keep a thermometer nearby to maintain the correct temperature for proper cooking.

Tongs. If you need to reach a lost dipper at the bottom of the pot, it is best to use tongs rather than your fondue fork.

Wine, beer, or cocktail glasses. Wine is the traditional beverage served with fondue, but your guests may enjoy any beverage of their choosing. It is best to avoid drinking water when serving cheese fondue, as water can make the cheese feel very heavy in your stomach.

FONDUES AND DON'TS

Set the right scene, fill your fondue pot with something delicious, and consider these tips, tricks, and traditions as a guideline for hosting a successful fondue party.

- Set your dippers and sauces on the table at least 30 minutes before you plan to eat so that they have a chance to come up to room temperature. Cold dippers and sauces aren't pleasant to consume with hot fondue.

- It's tempting to eat directly off your long-handled fondue fork, but the prongs are very sharp, and the arm of the fork can get quite hot as it lingers over the fondue pot. It's best to remove your dipped food to your plate and use a regular fork for eating.

- It is recommended to swirl your dipper in a figure eight when dipping into a pot of cheese fondue to keep the hot cheese from clumping.

- It can be fun to place a wager at the start of the meal to determine a consequence when a dipper is lost in the bottom of the pot. One possible payback could be buying a round of drinks for the table if you're at a restaurant, but it can be anything the group agrees on.

- Traditional cheese fondue is served with a shot of Kirschwasser halfway through the meal. This aids in the digestion of the heavy cheese, making room for more.

- A crust of toasted cheese called *la religieuse* (the nun) usually forms on the bottom of the fondue pot. The Swiss consider it a delicacy, so scrape it off and give it a try.

- Near the end of the meal, serve hot drinks like mint tea or mulled wine. Cheese fondue and dessert fondue can sit heavily in the stomach once they cool off, and a warmed liquid will aid in the digestion.

- Cheese fondue does not hold well, so preparing the fondue should be the last step once all dippers and side dishes are ready.

SAY CHEESE!

Your pot is a vessel for all different varieties of fondue, but it's best known for serving molten pots of melty, oozing cheese fondue. Choosing the right cheese is an essential part of your quest for cheese fondue nirvana. The following list of cheeses are all great for melting, but it is important to note that younger cheeses melt better than more aged cheeses because of their higher moisture content. Try to choose cheeses that are aged between 3 and 18 months for the best results. The cheeses and amounts listed in each recipe in this book are a guide that should be followed as closely as possible to achieve the desired result. Experimenting with different cheeses is a great way to discover what makes the perfect cheese fondue for you.

American. American cheese is a type of processed cheese made from a mixture of Colby, Cheddar, and other similar cheeses, often containing modified milk ingredients and stabilizers. Although whole-milk cheese is always a preferred choice, melted American cheese offers a smooth and creamy texture that is unique and useful in some recipes.

Appenzeller. A straw-colored, firm cow's milk cheese with small holes, this cheese is made in Switzerland. Appenzeller's bark is louder than its bite, with a pungent aroma yielding to a nutty, fruity, mild, and pleasing taste. A stronger flavor develops as the cheese ages, and this cheese can be used instead of Emmentaler.

Asiago. Asiago is a cow's milk cheese from Northern Italy that varies in texture from soft and pliable when young to firm and crumbly when very aged. Asiago Mezzano is aged for 3 to 8 months and is the best choice for melting. This cheese is tangy and nutty with a slight sweetness.

Beaufort. Beaufort is a firm Alpine-style cow's milk cheese from France made in very large wheels weighing up to 150 pounds. The beechwood hoops used to shape this cheese give it a distinctive, slightly concave rind, and the spruce wood shelves it is aged on give it a decidedly woodsy flavor. Use this cheese instead of Gruyère or Comté in any of your favorite cheese fondue recipes.

Brie. Different varieties of Brie are made and sold around the world, and most are appropriate for melting. The rind does not fully break down in the melting process, so it's best to remove the rind beforehand by scraping the edge of a spoon along the surface of the cheese until all the bloom has been removed. Brie will add a silky texture and buttery flavor to your fondue.

Cheddar. Cheddar is a firm cow's milk cheese that was originally made in England and can now be found from local producers around the world. White Cheddar is just the same as orange Cheddar, which is colored with annatto seed, a flavorless natural additive originally used to give the cheese more eye appeal. Whichever color you prefer, Cheddar melts best if it is aged for less than two years. It adds a rich and buttery, sharp tanginess to your fondue.

Comté. Comté is a firm, Alpine-style cow's milk cheese from France that is made in a similar style to Gruyère but with its own unique characteristics. Comté shows off flavors of wild herbs and roasted nuts with a pronounced savory profile. Comté can be used interchangeably with Gruyère as a foundation for all your favorite fondue recipes.

Edam. Edam is a semifirm cow's milk cheese originally made in Holland and now available commercially made around the world. Edam is typically sold in a ball with a wax coating to protect the cheese as it ages. This cheese is mild and buttery and melts into a smooth consistency.

Emmentaler. Made in massive 150-pound wheels, this pale-yellow cow's milk cheese is often referred to as Swiss cheese and is recognizable for its big round holes. The flavor is sweet and fruity, with a lingering tangy bite, and it is one of the greatest melting cheeses for fondue, mac and cheese, and vegetable gratin.

Fontina. Different varieties of Fontina cheese can be found around the world, but the original recipe is still made in the val d'Aosta region of Northern Italy. This semifirm Alpine-style cow's milk cheese is buttery and nutty and adds a silky texture to any dish that calls for melted cheese.

Gouda. Traditionally made in Holland, Gouda is a semifirm to firm cow's milk cheese, depending on how long it is aged. When young, Gouda is mild and buttery, with a cultured cream flavor. As Gouda ages, sweetness and nuttiness emerge as more distinct flavors. Choose a young Gouda for melting.

Gruyère. Gruyère is a firm Alpine-style cow's milk cheese from Switzerland aged for at least 6 to 9 months and made in 80-pound wheels. The paste is firm with a slightly grainy texture and a nutty, well-balanced sweet-and-salty taste, with notes of allium and cultured butter. Gruyère stands beside Emmentaler as an important melting cheese, and it makes for a great foundation for building the ultimate cheese fondue.

Havarti. Havarti is a semifirm cow's milk cheese originally made in Denmark. This cheese is considered a buttery, mild, and easy-going table cheese that the Danes commonly enjoy with most meals. Havarti is a rindless, higher-moisture cheese with an open texture that melts into a smooth consistency.

Monterey Jack. Monterey Jack is an original American cow's milk cheese with a firm texture and mild, buttery flavor. Today, Monterey Jack is a staple in Tex-Mex cuisine from the American Southwest and is often melted into burritos and Queso dip and used as a topping for enchiladas. Monterey Jack is an affordable melting cheese that will give you a moderately flavored, stringy cheese fondue.

Mozzarella. Mozzarella is a mild semifirm cow's milk cheese with a milky, buttery flavor. Fresh mozzarella does not melt properly for fondue, so look for pressed mozzarella not sold in brine. In fondue, mozzarella can become gummy, especially when over-stirred. I recommend using a small amount of mozzarella in your fondue to add body and a stringy consistency.

Provolone. Provolone is a firm pasta filata (stretched curd) cow's milk cheese that varies in taste depending on its age. When it is young, the flavor is soft and mild, making it a great cheese for melting on pizza. When it's aged, a stronger, piquant taste can be expected.

Raclette. Although raclette is most well known as a dish of melty cheese served over steamed potatoes, it is also a style of cheese. Raclette is a washed rind, semifirm cow's milk cheese traditionally made in the Savoie region of France. The flavors are smooth and buttery, with an interesting meaty note that comes from the rind. If you enjoy the flavor of the rind, try grating some of it into your fondue for a stronger taste.

St. Agur. St. Agur is a double-cream cow's milk blue cheese made in France. It's considered a "gateway cheese" for those who aren't sure if they like blue cheese. It's a mild blue cheese with an extra-creamy mouth feel. St. Agur will add a very tame blue cheese bite to your cheese fondue.

Stilton. Stilton is a semifirm cow's milk blue cheese made in a specific region in central England, in a large cylindrical shape called a truckle with a natural mottled rind. The texture of the paste is smooth and buttery, and the cheese has a distinct blue veining throughout. Stilton has a bold blue, meaty, earthy flavor.

Tallegio. Tallegio is a semisoft, washed rind cow's milk cheese from Northern Italy with a strong aroma. The taste is mild and buttery, with a pungent edge the longer the cheese is aged. It's best to remove the hard rind before melting for fondue.

Vacherin Fribourgeois. Similar to raclette, Vacherin Fribourgeois is a semifirm washed rind cow's milk cheese, but comes from the Fribourg region of Switzerland instead. This cheese is buttery and smooth, with a full-bodied meaty punch of flavor. The blush-colored rind adds an interesting character to your pot of cheese fondue.

AOC, DOP, AND WHY GOOD CHEESE MATTERS

It is important to choose the best-quality cheese for your budget when making fondue. Traditionally made cheese from whole milk offers layers of flavor that translate into a superior pot of cheese fondue. European cheeses often carry an AOC (Appellation d'origine Contrôlée) or DOP (Denominazione di Origine Protetta) certification. Both acronyms translate to "Protected Designation of Origin," meaning that the cheeses come from a specific geographical region or area and are made from a protected recipe that accounts for the care and feed of the animals, quality of milk, and specific parameters in the production and aging of the cheese. These symbols of excellence ensure that you are purchasing an authentic piece of cheese. Locally made cheeses are also a great choice, especially when they come from a reputable producer who practices natural cheesemaking. Look for cheeses made in the same style as the cheese listed in your recipe, and don't be afraid to experiment! Cheese fondue contains only a few simple ingredients, so take the time to choose cheese varieties that will produce the best possible pot.

TRADITIONAL SWISS FONDUE (PAGE 26)

3

cheese fondue

CHEESE FONDUE is a simple dish, consisting primarily of an emulsion of liquid and cheese, with a few supporting flavors for added character. There are different techniques for achieving a smooth, uniformly melted cheese fondue, but I recommend one technique over the rest: Allow the starch and liquid to thicken together before adding the cheese. Always add the cheese to the thickened liquid over a very low temperature, to avoid splitting your cheese fondue into an oily mess. Cut the rind off your cheese before grating, and bring to room temperature before melting.

CHEESY DIPPERS

Almost everything goes well with cheese, so the list of recommended dippers for cheese fondue is lengthy and includes beautiful breads, fresh and prepared vegetables, meats, seafood, and even creative combinations like precooked pierogi and ravioli. Select a minimum of three to four dippers to give your guests a well-rounded cheese fondue experience. These dippers can range from simple vegetables, meats, and seafood to more complex options like the homemade Gougères and Crostini recipes found in chapter 7. You can also get creative and invent your own cheesy dippers. Here are some ideas:

- Cubes of baguette, sourdough bread, rye bread, soft pretzels, naan, tortillas, tortilla chips, potato chips, hard pretzels, Garlic Bread Knots (page 156), ciabatta, focaccia, and Crostini (page 151)

- French fries, onion rings, hash brown potatoes, tater tots, mini pierogies, cheese-stuffed ravioli, and Gougères (page 152)

- Steamed or roasted vegetables, like mini potatoes, broccoli, cauliflower, carrots, Brussels sprouts, turnips, sweet potatoes, asparagus, and squash

- Fresh vegetables, like cherry tomatoes, cucumbers, peppers, and radishes

- Grilled vegetables, like zucchini, eggplant, peppers, mushrooms, and onions

- A selection of fruit, like grapes, plums, cubed apples, and pears

- Cured sliced meats, like *saucisson sec*, speck, smoked ham or turkey, smoked sausage, summer sausage, chorizo, Iberico ham, Serrano ham, rosette de Lyon, and Jambon de Paris

- Grilled shrimp, scallops, octopus, and canned Spanish mussels

- Pickled vegetable medley, pickled beets, olives, and cornichons

Traditional Swiss Fondue

SERVES 4 / PREP TIME: 10 MINUTES / **COOK TIME:** 15 MINUTES

The original recipe for Swiss cheese fondue was simply local wine and cheese melted together and served warm with cubes of fresh bread. Cornstarch, popularized in the early 1900s, created a smooth, consistent cheese fondue. This classic recipe will satisfy your desire for a pot of bubbling cheese fondue.

---

1 garlic clove, halved

¾ cup dry white wine, plus more
    as needed

8 ounces grated Gruyère cheese

8 ounces grated Emmentaler cheese

1 tablespoon cornstarch

Freshly squeezed lemon juice

1 tablespoon kirsch (optional)

Freshly ground black pepper

1. Rub the cut garlic clove around the inside of a medium saucepan. Discard the remaining clove. Pour in the wine and heat until almost boiling.
2. In a medium bowl, toss the cheeses with the cornstarch until evenly coated.
3. Add the cheese mixture slowly, stirring constantly. Continue stirring for 10 to 12 minutes, or until the cheese is melted into the hot wine and looks smooth and glossy.
4. Stir in lemon juice to taste and the kirsch (if using). Season with pepper.

5. Transfer to a fondue pot set to medium heat. If the fondue begins to thicken, add a splash of wine.

COOKING TIP: If your fondue splits and the cheese solids and liquids separate, stir in another teaspoon or two of lemon juice and whisk over very low heat. This will help bring it back together.

Moitié-Moitié Fondue

SERVES 4 / PREP TIME: 10 MINUTES / **COOK TIME:** 15 MINUTES

The French term *moitié-moitié* refers to a Swiss fondue made with half Gruyère cheese and half Vacherin Fribourgeois cheese and hails from the Fribourg canton of Switzerland. This cheese combination produces a luxuriously smooth texture, with an interesting, full-bodied flavor.

---

1 garlic clove, halved

¾ cup dry white wine, plus more as needed

8 ounces grated Gruyère cheese

8 ounces grated Vacherin Fribourgeois cheese

1 tablespoon cornstarch

Freshly squeezed lemon juice

1 tablespoon kirsch (optional)

Freshly ground black pepper

1. Rub the cut garlic clove around the inside of a medium saucepan. Discard the remaining clove. Pour in the wine and heat until almost boiling.
2. In a medium bowl, toss the cheeses with the cornstarch until evenly coated.
3. Add the cheese mixture to the hot wine slowly, stirring constantly. Continue stirring until all the cheese is melted and the fondue looks smooth and glossy, for 10 to 12 minutes.
4. Stir in lemon juice to taste and the kirsch (if using). Season with pepper.
5. Transfer to a fondue pot set to medium heat. If the fondue begins to thicken, add a splash of wine.

STORE-BOUGHT SHORTCUT: Traditional Swiss fondue kits are fast and easy, but buyer beware: They cost more and do not taste as good as homemade.

French Fondue

SERVES 4 / PREP TIME: 10 MINUTES / **COOK TIME:** 15 MINUTES

This recipe hails from the Jura Mountains of France, which are famous for their Comté. This hard cheese is similar to Gruyère, but it has its own robust medley of flavors and aromas. Beaufort, another French mountain cheese featured in this recipe, offers a buttery and herbaceous complexity.

---

1 garlic clove, halved

¾ cup dry white wine, plus more as needed

8 ounces grated 9-month aged Comté cheese

8 ounces grated Beaufort cheese

1 tablespoon cornstarch

Freshly squeezed lemon juice

1 tablespoon kirsch (optional)

Kosher salt

Freshly ground black pepper

1. Rub the cut garlic clove around the inside of a medium saucepan. Discard the remaining clove. Pour in the wine and heat until almost boiling.
2. In a medium bowl, toss the cheeses with the cornstarch until evenly coated.
3. Add the cheese mixture to the hot wine slowly, stirring constantly. Continue stirring until all the cheese is melted and the fondue looks smooth and glossy, for 10 to 12 minutes.
4. Stir in lemon juice to taste and the kirsch (if using). Season with salt and pepper.
5. Transfer to a fondue pot set to medium heat. If the fondue begins to thicken, add a splash of wine.

COOKING TIP: Grated fresh nutmeg is a delightful addition to this fondue—but only a little. Too much overpowers the taste of the cheese.

Italian Fonduta

SERVES 4 TO 6 / PREP TIME: 10 MINUTES / **COOK TIME:** 15 TO 20 MINUTES

Northern Italy is the home of Fontina val d'Aosta, an excellent melting cheese with a semifirm texture and a nutty, buttery flavor. This recipe is thickened with egg yolks instead of cornstarch, which makes this Italian-style fondue more like a rich custard sauce that's perfect for dipping ciabatta bread.

---

2 tablespoons salted butter

¾ cup whole milk, plus more
    as needed

¼ cup heavy (whipping) cream

5 large egg yolks

1 pound grated Fontina val
    d'Aosta cheese

1. In a medium saucepan, heat the butter, milk, and cream over medium heat to just below a simmer. Reduce the heat to low.
2. In a medium bowl, whisk the egg yolks together, then whisk in a ladleful of the hot milk mixture. Repeat 2 more times.
3. Pour the egg mixture back into the saucepan. Cook over low heat, whisking until the mixture thickens and coats the back of a spoon, for 5 to 7 minutes.
4. Remove from the heat and whisk in the Fontina cheese.
5. Transfer to a fondue pot set to medium heat. If the fondue begins to thicken, add a splash of milk.

COOKING TIP: Be careful not to overheat the egg and milk mixture, as the eggs can scramble. Remember, too low is better than too high.

Spanish Fondue

SERVES 2 TO 4 / PREP TIME: 10 MINUTES **/ COOK TIME:** 15 MINUTES

The flavors of Spain come to life in this bubbling pot of Manchego cheese fondue, with the aroma of smoked sweet paprika and spicy crumbled chorizo. Manchego is a sheep's milk cheese that adds a buttery richness to this fondue and is also a great match for rich seafood like shrimp and mussels.

---

1 (8-ounce) uncured chorizo, removed from the casing

1 cup dry white wine, plus more as needed

1 teaspoon freshly squeezed lemon juice

1 garlic clove, minced

⅛ teaspoon smoked sweet paprika

4 teaspoons cornstarch

12 ounces grated 3-month aged Manchego cheese

4 ounces grated Fontina cheese

Thinly sliced scallions, for garnish (optional)

1. In a small sauté pan, crumble the chorizo and cook over medium heat until the fat renders out and the meat is browned and cooked through. Drain and set aside.
2. In a medium saucepan, bring the wine, lemon juice, garlic, smoked paprika, and cornstarch to a simmer over medium heat until thickened. Reduce the heat to very low.

CONTINUED >

3. Add the cheeses to the hot wine mixture, and stir until the cheese melts and the fondue is smooth.

4. Transfer to a fondue pot set to medium heat. Top with the chorizo and scallions (if using) and serve immediately. If the fondue begins to thicken, add a splash of wine.

COOKING TIP: Manchego cheese aged for more than 3 to 6 months will not melt properly. You can use all Fontina cheese instead, although the results will not taste the same.

Truffle Fondue

SERVES 2 TO 4 / PREP TIME: 10 MINUTES / **COOK TIME:** 15 MINUTES

If you love black truffles, this irresistible fondue will keep you dipping until the very last drop. This recipe features two great Italian melting cheeses—Fontina and Tallegio—that produce a velvety, decadent fondue.

¾ cup dry white wine, plus more as needed

1 tablespoon cornstarch

10 ounces grated Fontina cheese

6 ounces cubed Tallegio cheese

1 teaspoon freshly squeezed lemon juice

2 tablespoons black truffle tartufata mushroom purée

1. In a medium saucepan, whisk the wine and cornstarch together. Bring to a simmer over medium heat until thickened. Reduce the heat to very low.
2. In a medium bowl, toss together the cheeses. Slowly add the cheeses to the saucepan and stir until the cheese melts and the fondue is smooth. Stir in the lemon juice and black truffle tartufata.
3. Transfer to a fondue pot set to medium heat. If the fondue begins to thicken, add a splash of wine.

COOKING TIP: Tartufata is available in specialty markets and on the Internet, but if you cannot locate it, substitute 1 teaspoon of black truffle oil or 2 ounces of black truffle–flavored cheese.

Hot Queso Fondue

SERVES 2 TO 4 / PREP TIME: 10 MINUTES / **COOK TIME:** 15 MINUTES

The Tex-Mex origins of Queso Fundido and hot Queso dip straddle the border of the Southern United States and Northern Mexico. Although these two hot cheese dips differ in many ways—one is simply cheese and chiles melted in a hot skillet, and the other is a creamy mixture of cheeses and roasted poblanos—they share many of the same flavors. This recipe combines the best qualities of both dishes into one hot and oozy creamy cheese fondue, with garnishes of chorizo, chiles, fresh cilantro, and tomatoes.

2 tablespoons tequila

¾ cup light beer, plus more
  as needed

1 garlic clove, minced

1 tablespoon cornstarch

½ cup American cheese

10 ounces grated Monterey
  Jack cheese

3 ounces grated Oaxaca cheese

½ cup crumbled chorizo, fried
  until crispy

¼ cup roasted green chile peppers,
  drained and chopped

2 tablespoons fresh cilantro, chopped

2 tablespoons seeded and
  diced tomato

1. In a medium saucepan, combine the tequila, beer, garlic, and cornstarch. Bring to a simmer over medium heat and whisk until thickened, for about 5 minutes. Reduce the heat to low.
2. Add the American cheese and whisk until it melts.
3. Add the Monterey Jack and Oaxaca cheeses and whisk until the cheeses are melted.

4. Transfer to a fondue pot set to medium heat. Garnish with the fried chorizo, chiles, cilantro, and tomato. If the fondue begins to thicken, add a splash of beer.

COOKING TIP: Oaxaca cheese is widely available in Latin markets around the world, but if you can't locate it, substitute mozzarella cheese.

Indian Masala Fondue

SERVES 2 TO 4 / PREP TIME: 10 MINUTES / **COOK TIME:** 15 MINUTES

Toasty warm spices like cumin, coriander, fennel seed, and turmeric make up the famous masala spice blend. These flavors are delicious paired with onion and a blend of Cheddar and Gouda cheeses. Serve this spice-infused cheese fondue with naan, a medley of steamed vegetables, and grilled meats like lamb and beef.

---

1 tablespoon salted butter

½ small Spanish onion, minced

1 tablespoon masala
    spice paste

¾ cup beer, plus more as needed

1 tablespoon cornstarch

10 ounces grated 1-year aged
    white Cheddar cheese

6 ounces grated mild Gouda cheese

1 tablespoon honey

1. In a sauté pan, heat the butter and onion and sweat over medium heat until tender and translucent, for about 7 minutes. Add the masala paste and sauté for 2 minutes. Set aside.
2. In a medium saucepan, whisk together the beer and cornstarch. Bring to a simmer over medium heat until thickened. Reduce the heat to very low.
3. In a small bowl, toss together the Cheddar and Gouda cheeses, and add them to the beer mixture. Stir the cheese until fully melted and the fondue is smooth, then add the onion mixture and honey.

4. Transfer to a fondue pot set
    to medium heat. If the fondue
    begins to thicken, add a splash
    of beer.

COOKING TIP: If masala spice paste
is not available to you, you can substitute 1 teaspoon of garam masala
and ¼ teaspoon of turmeric.

Basil Pesto Fondue

SERVES 2 TO 4 / PREP TIME: 10 MINUTES / **COOK TIME:** 10 MINUTES

Basil pesto is an herbaceous mix of nuts, garlic, Parmesan, and fresh basil that adds a punch of refreshing flavor to an otherwise heavy dish. This fondue is particularly suited for dipping precooked ravioli and tortellini and a selection of fresh and lightly grilled vegetables.

---

2 cups fresh basil leaves

2 garlic cloves, crushed

¼ cup extra-virgin olive oil

2 tablespoons pine nuts, toasted

2 tablespoons Parmesan cheese

2 teaspoons freshly squeezed lemon juice, divided

Kosher salt

Freshly ground black pepper

1 cup dry white wine or chicken stock, plus more as needed

4 teaspoons cornstarch

8 ounces grated Gruyère cheese

8 ounces grated Fontina cheese

1. Put the basil, garlic, olive oil, pine nuts, Parmesan cheese, and 1 teaspoon of lemon juice into a food processor. Process until the mixture forms a smooth paste. Season with salt and pepper. Set aside.
2. In a saucepan, combine the wine and cornstarch and bring to just below a simmer.
3. Add the cheeses to the hot, thickened wine, and stir over medium-low heat until the cheese melts and the fondue is smooth. Add the remaining teaspoon of lemon juice and 2 tablespoons of pesto and stir.

4. Transfer to a fondue pot set to medium heat. If the fondue begins to thicken, add a splash of wine.

STORE-BOUGHT SHORTCUT: Freshness is the key to good pesto. Skip the jarred stuff and look for brands in the refrigerated section for maximum flavor.

French Onion Fondue

SERVES 2 TO 4 / PREP TIME: 10 MINUTES / **COOK TIME:** 25 MINUTES

Classic French onion soup is famous for its warm, melty cheese and rich caramelized onion broth. This recipe brings those flavors together into a tasty cheese fondue. Serve with a Burgundian red wine for the full French bistro experience, and don't forget lots of fresh baguettes for dipping.

---

1 tablespoon salted butter

1 tablespoon extra-virgin olive oil

1 small Spanish onion,
   thinly sliced

1 teaspoon chopped fresh thyme

1 teaspoon brown sugar

Kosher salt

Freshly ground black pepper

1 cup dry white wine, plus more
   as needed

10 ounces grated Comté cheese

6 ounces grated raclette cheese

4 teaspoons cornstarch

Freshly squeezed lemon juice

2 teaspoons Cognac or sherry
   (optional)

1. In a small sauté pan, heat the butter and the olive oil over medium heat until the butter has melted. Add the onion, thyme, brown sugar, and salt and pepper to taste, and sauté until the onion is soft and golden brown, for about 15 minutes. Remove from the heat.

2. In a medium saucepan, bring the wine to just below a simmer over medium-low heat.

3. In a medium bowl, toss the cheeses with the cornstarch until evenly coated.

4. Add the cheese mixture to the hot wine and stir until the cheese melts and the fondue is smooth. Add lemon juice to taste and the Cognac (if using).
5. Stir in the caramelized onion.
6. Transfer to a fondue pot set to medium heat. If the fondue begins to thicken, add a splash of wine.

COOKING TIP: Keep your fondue warm on low heat. If it boils, it can separate into an oily mess.

Baked Brie Fondue

SERVES 2 TO 4 / PREP TIME: 10 MINUTES / **COOK TIME:** 10 MINUTES

Combine the sweet and savory flavors of a classic baked Brie dish by adding fig jam and smoky bacon to this rich fondue. Serve this decadent Brie fondue with an array of sweet and savory dippers like grapes and apples, baguettes, and steamed squash and potatoes.

¾ cup dry white wine, plus more
    as needed

1 tablespoon cornstarch

1 pound Brie cheese, rind removed
    and cut into ¼-inch cubes

¼ cup fig jam

¼ cup crumbled, cooked bacon

1. In a medium saucepan, whisk the wine and cornstarch together. Bring to a simmer over medium heat until thickened, then reduce the heat to low.
2. Add the Brie cheese one handful at a time, stirring constantly until smooth.
3. Stir in the fig jam and crumbled bacon.
4. Transfer to a fondue pot set to medium heat. If the fondue begins to thicken, add a splash of wine.

COOKING TIP: Remove the rind by dragging the edge of a spoon along the surface of the Brie, pressing down on the back of the spoon just enough to lift the thin rind away from the cheese.

Canadian Maple-Bacon Fondue

SERVES 2 TO 4 / PREP TIME: 10 MINUTES / **COOK TIME:** 15 MINUTES

Nothing can replace the sweet and woodsy flavor of pure maple syrup, an iconic match for smoky bacon. Aged white Cheddar pulls all these flavors together into a savory cheese fondue that's perfect for your next weekend brunch menu. Serve with roasted sweet potatoes, mini pancakes, and breakfast sausage.

¾ cup milk, plus more as needed

1 tablespoon cornstarch

12 ounces grated 1-year aged white Cheddar cheese

4 ounces grated mild Gouda cheese

¼ cup pure maple syrup

4 bacon slices, cooked and finely chopped

Freshly ground black pepper

1. In a medium saucepan, combine the milk and cornstarch. Bring to a simmer over medium heat and whisk until thickened. Reduce the heat to low.
2. Add the cheeses to the hot milk and stir until the cheese melts and the fondue is smooth.
3. Stir in the maple syrup and bacon. Season with pepper.
4. Transfer to a fondue pot set to medium heat. If the fondue begins to thicken, add a splash of milk.

COOKING TIP: Low heat is the key to prevent your milk mixture from turning grainy. Never bring milk and cheese to a boil.

American Cheeseburger Fondue

SERVES 2 TO 4 / PREP TIME: 10 MINUTES / **COOK TIME:** 15 MINUTES

This recipe combines all the components of a classic American cheeseburger into a hot cheese fondue that kids and grown-ups alike will love. Dill pickles are an optional add-in to the finished fondue, or you can serve them on the side. Use this recipe as a topping for French fries or a baked potato if you're feeling adventurous.

1 tablespoon extra-virgin olive oil

¼ cup minced white onion

1 garlic clove, minced

8 ounces lean ground beef

1 teaspoon prepared yellow mustard

1 teaspoon hamburger seasoning

¾ cup chicken stock, plus more as needed

1 tablespoon cornstarch

6 ounces American cheese

8 ounces grated sharp Cheddar cheese

⅓ cup dill pickles, finely diced (optional)

Freshly ground black pepper

1. In a sauté pan, heat the olive oil over medium heat. Add the onion and garlic and cook for 2 minutes.
2. Add the ground beef, yellow mustard, and hamburger seasoning. Sauté until the meat is fully cooked and browned. Drain off any excess fat.
3. In a saucepan, bring the chicken stock and cornstarch to a simmer over medium heat and whisk until thickened. Reduce the heat to low.
4. Add the American cheese and whisk until it melts.

5. Add the Cheddar cheese and stir until it is melted. Add the ground beef, dill pickles (if using), and pepper to taste.
6. Transfer to a fondue pot set to medium heat. If the fondue begins to thicken, add a splash of chicken stock.

COOKING TIP: Hamburger seasoning usually contains paprika, onion powder, garlic powder, brown sugar, salt, pepper, and oregano. Alternately, make a blend that suits your taste.

Cheddar and Ale Fondue

SERVES 2 TO 4 / PREP TIME: 10 MINUTES / **COOK TIME:** 10 MINUTES

The sharp and tangy bite of an aged Cheddar plays well with malty English ale in this rich and hearty fondue. Worcestershire sauce, mustard, and Tabasco give added heft, making it ideal for colder weather. Serve with a mixture of steamed vegetables and potatoes for dipping and a tangy fruit chutney to help cut through the richness of the fondue.

¾ **cup English-style ale, plus more as needed**

1 **tablespoon cornstarch**

12 **ounces grated 1-year aged white Cheddar cheese**

4 **ounces grated mild Gouda cheese**

1 **teaspoon spicy brown mustard**

1 **teaspoon Worcestershire sauce**

1 **teaspoon Tabasco hot sauce**

1. In a saucepan, bring the ale and cornstarch to a simmer over medium heat and whisk until thickened. Reduce the heat to low.
2. Add the cheeses to the hot beer mixture. Stir until the cheese melts and the fondue is smooth, then add the mustard, Worcestershire, and Tabasco.
3. Transfer to a fondue pot set to medium heat. If the fondue begins to thicken, add a splash of beer.

COOKING TIP: Nonalcoholic beer is available in the grocery store and makes for a good substitute for regular beer in this recipe.

Blue Cheese and Leek Fondue

SERVES 2 TO 4 / PREP TIME: 10 MINUTES / **COOK TIME:** 15 MINUTES

Cheddar cheese and mild Gouda form a rich and creamy foundation, and a liberal crumble of blue cheese is added on top. Pair with a pint or two of malty stout to be transported to a pub in the British countryside.

---

1 large leek, green leaves removed, cleaned and diced

1 tablespoon salted butter

¾ cup beer, plus more as needed

1 tablespoon cornstarch

10 ounces grated 1-year aged white Cheddar cheese

6 ounces grated mild Gouda cheese

1 teaspoon Worcestershire sauce

2 ounces strong blue cheese, crumbled

1. In a sauté pan, sweat the leek in butter over medium heat until very soft but not browned, for about 8 minutes. Set aside.
2. In a medium saucepan, bring the beer and cornstarch to a simmer over medium heat and whisk until thickened. Reduce the heat to low.
3. Add the Cheddar and Gouda cheeses to the hot beer mixture and stir until the cheese melts and the fondue is smooth. Stir in the leek and Worcestershire sauce.
4. Transfer to a fondue pot set to medium heat. Garnish the top of the fondue with the crumbled blue cheese. If the fondue begins to thicken, add a splash of beer.

COOKING TIP: Use leftover blue cheese and leek fondue as a topping for scalloped potatoes. Finish under the broiler for a crispy blue cheese crust on top of the potatoes.

Pimento Cheese Fondue

SERVES 2 TO 4 / PREP TIME: 10 MINUTES / **COOK TIME:** 10 MINUTES

Pimento cheese spread is a delicacy in the Southern United States that works beautifully when transformed into bubbling pots of fondue. All the classic flavors of pimento cheese are here: sharp Cheddar, garlic, hot sauce, and pickled roasted pimento. Take your fondue one step further by serving homemade buttermilk biscuits for dipping.

½ cup milk

3 teaspoons cornstarch, divided

¼ cup dry white wine, plus more as needed

1 garlic clove, minced

½ cup cream cheese

1 teaspoon Dijon or whole-grain mustard

10 ounces grated sharp orange Cheddar cheese

⅓ cup pimentos, drained well and chopped

1 teaspoon Louisiana-style hot sauce

Freshly ground black pepper

1. In a medium saucepan, bring the milk and 2 teaspoons of cornstarch to a simmer over medium heat.
2. In a small bowl, mix the wine, garlic, and remaining 1 teaspoon of cornstarch. Add it to the milk mixture. Simmer until thickened, then reduce the heat to low.
3. Add the cream cheese and mustard and whisk until the cheese is melted.
4. Add the Cheddar cheese and stir until it is melted.

5. Add the pimentos and hot sauce. Season with pepper.
6. Transfer to a fondue pot set to medium heat. If the fondue begins to thicken, add a splash of wine.

COOKING TIP: If you like spicy pimento cheese, add ¼ teaspoon of cayenne pepper and garnish with chopped pickled jalapeño peppers.

Fondue in a Pumpkin

SERVES 4 TO 6 / PREP TIME: 10 MINUTES **/ COOK TIME:** 1 HOUR

A whole roasted pumpkin doubles as an edible fondue pot and is a deliciously showy way to present your cheese fondue. Choose a fondue recipe that complements the flavors of the roasted pumpkin, like the French Onion Fondue (page 40) or the Wild Mushroom and Herb Fondue (page 55).

---

1 (2-pound) pumpkin

2 tablespoons extra-virgin olive oil

Kosher salt

Freshly ground black pepper

Prepared pot of fondue

1. Preheat the oven to 400°F. Wash and pat dry the pumpkin. Cut off the top and stem of the pumpkin to make a lid. Scoop out and discard the seeds and loose flesh.
2. Drizzle the inside of the pumpkin and the underside of the lid with the olive oil. Season with salt and pepper.
3. Place the pumpkin and lid on a parchment paper–lined baking sheet and roast for about 45 minutes. The pumpkin is done when the flesh is soft all the way through when poked with a fork and the cut edge is caramelized.
4. As the pumpkin bakes, prepare enough fondue to fill the pumpkin. A double-batch of fondue should fill a 2-pound pumpkin.
5. Place the roasted pumpkin on a serving plate or dish. Pour in fondue, place the lid on, and transfer the pumpkin to the table.

COOKING TIP: Serve the fondue in a smaller, personal-size squash or pumpkin. Look for half-pound acorn squash or mini pumpkins, and reduce roasting time as needed. Ladle a scoop of fondue into each pumpkin, and serve with a baguette for dipping.

Cacio e Pepe Fondue

SERVES 2 TO 4 / PREP TIME: 10 MINUTES / **COOK TIME:** 10 MINUTES

Cacio e Pepe is a Roman dish traditionally made with Pecorino Romano, a sheep's milk cheese with a strong, salty, piquant bite. This blend of Pecorino Romano, Fontina, and cream cheese forms a creamy fondue that's perfect for dipping an endless array of vegetables, precooked pasta, and homemade Crostini (page 151).

¾ cup dry white wine, plus more as needed

1 tablespoon cornstarch

½ cup cream cheese

8 ounces grated Pecorino Romano cheese

4 ounces grated Fontina cheese

1 to 2 teaspoons freshly ground black pepper

1. In a medium saucepan, bring the wine and cornstarch to a simmer over medium heat and whisk until thickened. Reduce the heat to low.
2. Add the cream cheese and whisk until it is melted.
3. Add the Pecorino Romano and Fontina cheeses and stir until the cheeses melt and the fondue is smooth. Add the pepper to taste.
4. Transfer to a fondue pot set to medium heat. If the fondue begins to thicken, add a splash of wine.

COOKING TIP: Add a clove of minced garlic to this sauce and toss with pasta for an excellent alfredo sauce. If the dish gets too thick, add a splash of pasta water or wine.

Spinach and Artichoke Fondue

SERVES 4 TO 6 / PREP TIME: 15 MINUTES / **COOK TIME:** 10 MINUTES

Spinach and artichoke dip quickly became a favorite snack in the 1950s. This recipe combines marinated artichoke hearts, cooked spinach, and garlic with a blend of four cheeses that form an irresistibly cheesy fondue.

¾ **cup dry white wine, plus more as needed**

2 **garlic cloves, minced**

1 **tablespoon cornstarch**

½ **cup cream cheese**

8 **ounces grated Monterey Jack cheese**

6 **ounces grated mozzarella cheese**

2 **ounces grated Parmesan cheese**

¼ **cup cooked spinach, squeezed dry and chopped**

½ **cup marinated artichoke hearts, drained and chopped**

Freshly ground black pepper

1. In a saucepan, bring the wine, garlic, and cornstarch to a simmer over medium heat and whisk until thickened. Reduce the heat to low.
2. Add the cream cheese and whisk until it is melted.
3. In a medium bowl, toss together the Monterey Jack, mozzarella, and Parmesan cheeses, then add them to the wine mixture and stir until the cheeses melt and the fondue is smooth.

CONTINUED >

CHEESE FONDUE

4. Add the spinach and artichoke hearts to the fondue and stir to combine. Season with pepper. Allow all the ingredients to heat through until everything is very warm but not bubbling.

5. Transfer to a fondue pot set to medium heat. If the fondue begins to thicken, add a splash of wine.

COOKING TIP: Make sure your spinach and artichoke hearts are well drained. Any excess water will thin out the fondue and could make it runny.

Wild Mushroom and Herb Fondue

SERVES 2 TO 4 / PREP TIME: 10 MINUTES / **COOK TIME:** 15 MINUTES

Mushrooms and herbs are the perfect savory partner for melting cheeses like the Gruyère and Fontina featured in this recipe. If you have access to a selection of dried mushrooms like porcinis and chanterelles, simply steep them in hot water for 5 to 10 minutes and drain well before adding them to the other mushrooms. This recipe also makes for a delicious sauce for pasta or grilled vegetables.

---

2 tablespoons extra-virgin olive oil

2 cups mixed cremini, oyster, and shiitake mushrooms, cleaned and cut into ½-inch slices

1 teaspoon fresh rosemary, chopped

1½ teaspoons fresh thyme, chopped

¼ cup fresh parsley leaves, chopped

Kosher salt

Freshly ground black pepper

¾ cup dry white wine, plus more as needed

10 ounces grated Gruyère cheese

6 ounces grated Fontina cheese

4 teaspoons cornstarch

Freshly squeezed lemon juice

1. In a medium sauté pan, warm the olive oil over medium-high heat for 1 to 2 minutes until very hot. Add the mushrooms and sauté until cooked through and browned, for about 6 minutes.

2. Add the rosemary, thyme, and parsley and season with salt and pepper. Sauté for 2 minutes and remove from the heat.

CONTINUED >

3. In a medium saucepan, bring the wine to just below a simmer over medium heat.
4. In a medium bowl, toss the cheeses with the cornstarch until evenly coated.
5. Add the cheese mixture to the wine and stir until the cheeses melt and the fondue is smooth. Add lemon juice to taste.
6. Stir in the mushrooms.
7. Transfer to a fondue pot set to medium heat. If the fondue begins to thicken, add a splash of wine.

COOKING TIP: Chicken or vegetable broth is a great alternative to wine here. Add the lemon juice to the broth as it heats up to help the cheese emulsify.

Jalapeño Popper Fondue

SERVES 2 TO 4 / PREP TIME: 10 MINUTES / **COOK TIME:** 40 MINUTES

Spicy jalapeño peppers, smoky crisp bacon, and melty Monterey Jack cheese hit all the right notes for a timeless combination that will become a favorite for you and your guests. Serve this fondue with everything from tortilla chips to steamed broccoli—even tater tots.

---

4 or 5 jalapeño peppers

1 teaspoon extra-virgin olive oil

1 garlic clove, minced

½ cup milk, plus more as needed

¼ cup heavy (whipping) cream

1 tablespoon cornstarch

12 ounces grated Monterey Jack cheese

2 ounces grated mozzarella cheese

½ cup cream cheese

4 bacon slices, cooked crispy, chopped

Pinch kosher salt

Freshly ground black pepper

1. Preheat the oven to 400°F.
2. In a bowl, toss the peppers with olive oil and transfer to a baking sheet. Roast in the oven until tender, for about 40 minutes. Allow to rest until cooled. Remove and discard the stem, skin, and seeds, then finely chop the flesh and set aside.
3. In a medium saucepan, bring the garlic, milk, cream, and cornstarch to a simmer over medium heat and whisk until thickened. Reduce the heat to very low.

CONTINUED >

4. Add the Monterey Jack and mozzarella cheeses and stir until the cheeses melt and the fondue is smooth.
5. Add the cream cheese and stir until it is melted. Stir in the roasted peppers and bacon. Season with salt and pepper.
6. Transfer to a fondue pot set to medium heat. If the fondue begins to thicken, add a splash of milk.

COOKING TIP: If you can find roasted jalapeño or poblano peppers in a jar, you can substitute those for the ones in this recipe. Make sure to drain any excess liquid before adding them to the fondue.

ASIAN TEMPURA FONDUE (PAGE 66)

4

fondue bourguignonne

HOT OIL fondue is a delicious way to quickly cook tender cuts of meat and seafood, vegetables, and crispy tempura-battered foods. It's important to ensure that your oil maintains a temperature of 350° to 375°F, which will quickly cook a thin slice of meat or fish or a whole shrimp or scallop in about 3 minutes. Tempura-battered items are ready when they float on top of the oil and have a light golden brown color and crispy coating. Serve your hot oil fondue with an array of sauces to add flavor and complete the meal.

HOT OIL FONDUE DIPPERS

Hot oil fondue typically calls for meat and hearty seafood, so focus on quality cuts of your favorites, from beef and venison to shrimp and salmon. People who don't eat meat can enjoy this fondue style, too; consider tempura-fried vegetables like sweet potatoes and pearl onions, cubed tofu, or melty Halloumi cheese. Select a minimum of three or four meat, seafood, and vegetable dippers to offer your guests a well-rounded meal. More inventive ideas like spring rolls and mini meatballs are fun to eat and pair well with a variety of sauces found in chapter 7.

- Cubed or sliced raw beef, veal, lamb, venison, bison, pork, chicken, turkey, and duck

- Breaded schnitzel-style slices of chicken, pork, veal, beef, or turkey

- Mini meatballs or sausage bites like bratwurst, knockwurst, frankfurter, or Weisswurst

- Cubed salmon, cod, tilapia, snapper, white fish, and fish balls

- Cleaned and prepared shrimp, scallops, calamari, lobster, and crab

- Cubed tofu and Halloumi cheese

- Steamed mini potatoes, broccoli, cauliflower, carrots, potatoes, sweet potatoes, Brussels sprouts, pearl onions, and squash

- Raw mushrooms, zucchini, peppers, scallions, and artichokes

- Potato hash browns, mini pierogies, dumplings, spring rolls, wontons, and precooked ravioli

Classic Bourguignonne Hot Oil Fondue

SERVES 4 / PREP TIME: 20 MINUTES / **COOK TIME:** 2 TO 4 MINUTES

Classic fondue Bourguignonne originally featured cubes of beef for frying and was served alongside a selection of sauces and a refreshing green salad. Use the following list of sauces, along with some of your favorite dippers, to create an interesting meal with an array of flavors.

---

2 pounds cubed or sliced raw meats, like beef, lamb, pork, chicken, turkey, and mixed seafood

3 or 4 additional dippers of your choice

Sauces of your choice

6 cups peanut, safflower, or sunflower oil

Kosher salt

1. Prepare a selection of dippers and sauces with a variety of textures and flavors. Arrange them around the fondue pot.
2. Pour the oil into the fondue pot and bring it to a temperature hot enough for frying, about 350°F.
3. Skewer your chosen item on a fondue fork and place it in the oil. Once the item is cooked through, slide it off the fondue fork and onto a plate. Season with salt and sauces. (Remember not to eat off the fondue fork. It gets hot!)

RECOMMENDED SAUCES: Béarnaise Sauce (page 122), Rouille Sauce (page 133), Steak Sauce (page 120), Tartar Sauce (page 125), Mayonnaise (page 126), Curry Aioli (page 128), Horseradish Cream (page 129), and Roquefort Dip (page 130)

Bagna Cauda Fondue

SERVES 4 / PREP TIME: 10 MINUTES / **COOK TIME:** 20 MINUTES

This oil-based fondue dish is not served hot for frying but is rather like a warm bath for soaking poached shrimp and tender grilled beef, roasted vegetables, and peppery fresh radishes. This flavorful anchovy-laced fondue is best served when the sun is hot and the drinks are refreshing.

1 cup milk

8 to 10 whole garlic cloves

1 cup extra-virgin olive oil

3 ounces oil-packed anchovy fillets

Freshly ground black pepper

2 pounds thinly sliced grilled or roasted meats like beef, lamb, pork, chicken, turkey, and mixed seafood

3 or 4 additional dippers of your choice

1. In a small saucepan, combine the milk and garlic and bring to a gentle simmer over medium heat for 7 to 8 minutes, or until the garlic is just softened.
2. Drain the garlic well, and discard the milk.
3. Wipe out the saucepan, then return the garlic to the saucepan and cover with the olive oil. Cook over low heat for about 10 minutes, or until the garlic is soft enough that it can be mashed into the oil with the back of a spoon.
4. Add the anchovies and cook, stirring and mashing, until they have fully dissolved into the sauce along with the garlic, forming a thick sauce. Season with pepper to taste.

5. Transfer to a fondue pot over low heat and serve immediately with the precooked meats and dippers.

TIP: Serve with a selection of Italian cheeses on the side for a more authentic experience.

Asian Tempura Fondue

SERVES 4 / PREP TIME: 20 MINUTES / **COOK TIME:** 2 TO 4 MINUTES

Light and crispy tempura batter is perfect for frying bites of fresh seafood, thinly sliced meats, and crisp-tender steamed vegetables. Pre-steamed dumplings, meat-stuffed wontons, and mini spring rolls are a nice addition to this dish, and although they do not require the tempura batter coating, they do fry very quickly in the hot oil.

---

2 pounds cubed or sliced raw meats, like beef, lamb, pork, chicken, turkey, and mixed seafood

3 or 4 additional dippers of your choice

Sauces of your choice

Tempura Batter (page 142)

6 cups peanut, safflower, or sunflower oil

Kosher salt

1. Prepare a selection of dippers and sauces with a variety of textures and flavors. Arrange them around the fondue pot.
2. Prepare tempura batter and transfer it to a small bowl. Keep cold until ready to serve.
3. Pour the oil into the fondue pot and bring it to a temperature hot enough for frying, about 350°F.
4. Skewer your chosen item on a fondue fork. Dip the item into the tempura batter and twirl, making sure it is completely coated.

5. Place the battered item in the oil, remove the fork, and cook for 2 to 3 minutes, or until it's floating and fried on both sides. Set on paper towels to drain.
6. Season with salt and sauces and enjoy.

SAUCE TIP: Serve with Peanut Sauce (page 124), Vietnamese Nuoc Cham Sauce (page 131), and Korean Gochujang Ketchup (page 134). Sauces like hoisin, teriyaki, sweet-and-sour, and soy sauce are also great with this fondue.

Spanish-Style Oil Fondue

SERVES 4 / PREP TIME: 20 MINUTES, PLUS 30 MINUTES TO CHILL / **COOK TIME:** 2 TO 4 MINUTES

This recipe features crispy, fried cubes of melty Manchego cheese along with fresh chorizo. Serve with smoked paprika–infused homemade mayonnaise to marry these great Spanish flavors, and don't forget a pitcher of sangria to wash it all down.

¼ cup all-purpose flour

1 large egg

½ cup bread crumbs

8 ounces 6-month aged Manchego cheese, cut into ½-inch cubes

6 cups peanut, safflower, or sunflower oil

1 pound fresh chorizo, portioned into 1-inch pieces

Kosher salt

2 or 3 sauces of your choice

1. Put the flour, egg, and bread crumbs in 3 separate bowls. Beat the egg. One at a time, roll a cube of Manchego cheese in the flour, then the egg, and lastly the bread crumbs, creating a coating on all sides of the cheese. Repeat until all the cheese has been coated. Refrigerate for 30 minutes.

2. Pour the oil into the fondue pot and bring it to a temperature hot enough for frying, about 350°F.

3. Skewer a portion of chorizo or cheese cube on a fondue fork and slide it into the oil. Cook for 3 to 5 minutes, or until golden brown. Set on paper towels to drain.

4. Season with salt and sauces and enjoy.

SAUCE TIP: Serve with a selection of sauces like Rouille Sauce (page 133), Mayonnaise (page 126) mixed with ½ teaspoon smoked Spanish paprika, and lemon wedges. Look for sauces like Romesco or garlic aioli to serve with this fondue if homemade sauces are not an option.

Italian-Style Oil Fondue

SERVES 4 / PREP TIME: 20 MINUTES, PLUS 30 MINUTES TO CHILL / **COOK TIME:** 2 TO 4 MINUTES

Breaded mozzarella cubes and mini meatballs are the star of the show in this fun, Italian-inspired recipe. Pair them with classic Italian flavors like basil pesto and tomato marinara, along with a selection of vegetables, seafood, and precooked cheese-stuffed ravioli. Note: Don't use fresh mozzarella for this fondue, as it won't hold up to frying.

FOR THE MOZZARELLA CUBES

¼ cup all-purpose flour

1 large egg

½ cup bread crumbs

8 ounces mozzarella cheese, cut into ½-inch cubes

Kosher salt

FOR THE MINI MEATBALLS

8 ounces ground beef

8 ounces ground pork

¼ cup Italian bread crumbs

½ teaspoon Italian seasoning

1 large egg

Kosher salt

Freshly ground black pepper

FOR THE FONDUE

3 or 4 additional dippers of your choice

Sauces of your choice

6 cups peanut, safflower, or sunflower oil

Kosher salt

TO MAKE THE MOZZARELLA CUBES

1. Put the flour, egg, and bread crumbs in 3 separate bowls. Beat the egg.
2. Roll a cube of mozzarella cheese in the flour, then the egg, and lastly the bread crumbs, creating a coating on all sides of the cheese. Season with salt.
3. Repeat until all the cheese has been coated. Refrigerate for 30 minutes.

TO MAKE THE MINI MEATBALLS

4. In a medium bowl, mix the beef, pork, bread crumbs, Italian seasoning, and egg until just combined. Season with salt and pepper.
5. Measure 1 tablespoon of meat mixture and roll into a mini meatball shape. Repeat until all the mixture has been used.
6. Refrigerate until the fondue pot is ready for frying.

TO MAKE THE FONDUE

7. Prepare a selection of dippers and sauces with a variety of textures and flavors. Arrange them around the fondue pot.
8. Pour the oil into the fondue pot and bring it to a temperature hot enough for frying, about 350°F.
9. Skewer a meatball or cheese cube on a fondue fork and place it in the oil, removing the fork. Fry for 2 to 3 minutes, or until it is cooked through.
10. Season with salt and sauces and enjoy.

STORE-BOUGHT SHORTCUT: Mini breaded mozzarella sticks are a good substitute for breading your own mozzarella. Just make sure they aren't too big, or they will take too long to fry.

German-Style Oil Fondue

SERVES 4 / PREP TIME: 15 MINUTES / **COOK TIME:** 2 TO 4 MINUTES

This hot oil fondue comes together when it is served with steamed mini potatoes and a selection of traditional German condiments, like tangy sauerkraut, sweet-and-sour cabbage, and an array of mustards. Don't forget to serve your German fondue with a pint or two of Pilsner.

FOR THE SCHNITZEL

2 pounds thinly sliced boneless beef, veal, pork, chicken, or turkey

⅓ cup all-purpose flour

3 large eggs

2 cups seasoned bread crumbs

FOR THE FONDUE

3 or 4 additional dippers of your choice

Sauces of your choice

6 cups peanut, safflower, or sunflower oil

2 pounds breaded chicken, beef, veal, or pork schnitzel

Kosher salt

TO MAKE THE SCHNITZEL

1. Cut the thinly sliced meats into 4-inch pieces, no bigger than 2 to 3 bites each.
2. Put the flour, eggs, and bread crumbs in 3 separate bowls. Beat the eggs.

3. Dredge each piece of meat in the flour, shaking off any excess. Dip into the eggs, then dredge in the bread crumbs. Set the breaded meat aside on a plate and continue until all of the meat has been breaded. Keep cold until ready to fry.

TO MAKE THE FONDUE

4. Prepare a selection of dippers and sauces with a variety of textures and flavors. Arrange them around the fondue pot.
5. Pour the oil into the fondue pot and bring it to a temperature hot enough for frying, about 350°F.
6. Skewer the meat on a fondue fork and place it in the oil, removing the fork. Fry for 3 to 4 minutes, or until it is cooked through.
7. Season with salt and sauces and enjoy.

COOKING TIP: Serve with a selection of pickles, soft pretzels, and dark rye bread for a well-rounded German experience.

FONDUE BOURGUIGNONNE

Greek-Style Oil Fondue

SERVES 4 / PREP TIME: 20 MINUTES, PLUS 30 MINUTES TO MARINATE / **COOK TIME:** 2 TO 4 MINUTES

Greek cuisine is known for its fresh seafood, fried cheese, and souvlaki-style meats that lend themselves well to hot oil fondue cooking. Serve with a selection of Greek-style pita bread, herb-marinated olives, and garlicky dips and spreads to complement the quickly fried meats and Halloumi cheese.

⅓ cup extra-virgin olive oil

2 tablespoons red-wine vinegar

2 tablespoons freshly squeezed lemon juice

1 tablespoon fresh oregano leaves, chopped

1 garlic clove, minced

Freshly ground black pepper

2 pounds mixed thinly sliced meats, like beef, lamb, pork, chicken, turkey, seafood, and Halloumi cheese

3 or 4 additional dippers of your choice

Sauces of your choice

6 cups peanut, safflower, or sunflower oil

Kosher salt

1. In a bowl, mix together the olive oil, vinegar, lemon juice, oregano, garlic, and pepper to taste, and use as a marinade for the meat, seafood, and cheese dippers. Marinate for 30 minutes before frying.
2. Prepare a selection of dippers and sauces with a variety of textures and flavors. Arrange them around the fondue pot.
3. Add the oil to the fondue pot and bring it to a temperature hot enough for frying, about 350°F.

4. Skewer your chosen item on a fondue fork and place it in the oil, removing the fork. Fry for 2 to 3 minutes, or until it is cooked through.
5. Season with salt and sauces and enjoy.

SAUCE TIP: Serve with lemon wedges and a selection of sauces, like Tzatziki Sauce (page 132), olive oil mixed with lemon juice and oregano, and Mayonnaise (page 126) mixed with 1 or 2 minced garlic cloves.

TOMATO-SAFFRON BROTH FONDUE (PAGE 87)

5

fondue hot pot

HOT BROTH-STYLE fondue is enjoyed the world over.
Bubbling pots of boldly flavored broth are served to cook
a variety of raw meats, seafood, and vegetables.
Japanese Shabu Shabu and Chinese Hot Pot are traditionally served
with a small bowl of steamed rice for soaking up all the
nutrient-dense broth at the bottom of the pot, and a variety
of sauces for dipping the cooked meats and seafood.
Hot Pot is a healthy way of cooking that
nearly everyone can enjoy, regardless
of diet preferences.

HOT BROTH FONDUE DIPPERS

The versatile hot broth fondue pairs well with a variety of dippers that are complemented by the sauce options. Choose a minimum of three or four dippers from an array of thinly sliced meat, seafood, and vegetable options so your guests can experiment with different flavors and textures. Put a global spin on the broth base you choose by serving your hot broth with a side of European-influenced focaccia, ciabatta, Greek pita, and precooked pasta, or Asian-inspired steamed dumplings or noodles, for soaking up all the nutritious broth at the bottom of the pot. Here are some ideas for dippers:

- Thinly sliced raw beef, veal, lamb, venison, bison, duck, chicken, turkey, and pork

- Meatballs and bite-size sausage

- Cleaned and prepared raw shrimp, calamari, crab, lobster, fish balls, salmon, halibut, snapper, and cod

- Steamed or roasted mini potatoes, broccoli, cauliflower, carrots, artichoke hearts, potatoes, turnips, Brussels sprouts, sweet potatoes, and squash

- Grilled zucchini, asparagus, peppers, mushrooms, and eggplant

- Baguettes, sourdough bread, soft pretzels, focaccia, ciabatta, Greek pita bread, and ravioli

- Fried, firm, or silken tofu; Halloumi cheese

- Steamed dumplings, rice, or rice cakes; mung bean, soba, or rice noodles

- Chopped leafy Asian greens, cabbage, bok choy, mini corn, snow peas, and shiitake and enoki mushrooms

Classic Beef Broth Hot Pot

SERVES 4 / PREP TIME: 5 MINUTES / **COOK TIME:** 10 MINUTES

Rich and soothing homemade beef broth is the star of the show in this classic Hot Pot recipe. I recommend making a pot of homemade Classic Beef Broth (page 135) and adding enough salt so your dippers season as they cook. This basic recipe is a great foundation for exploring an array of interesting dippers and sauces.

---

8 cups Classic Beef Broth (page 135)

2 garlic cloves, crushed

1½ teaspoons kosher salt, plus more for seasoning

2 pounds cubed or sliced raw meats, like beef, lamb, bison, or venison

3 or 4 additional dippers of your choice

Sauces of your choice

1. In a medium saucepan, bring the broth, garlic, and salt to a simmer over medium heat.
2. Arrange the various dippers and sauces around the pot.
3. Transfer the hot broth to a fondue pot set to medium-high heat.
4. Skewer your chosen item on a fondue fork and place it in the hot broth. Once the item is cooked through, slide it off the fondue fork and onto a plate. Season with salt and sauces.

COOKING TIP: Make a double recipe of the broth and freeze it for future fondue meals.

Classic Chicken Broth Hot Pot

SERVES 4 / PREP TIME: 5 MINUTES / **COOK TIME:** 10 MINUTES

Good-quality chicken broth is vibrant and aromatic, and this simple recipe allows the natural flavors of the broth to shine. I recommend making a pot of Chicken Broth for this recipe (page 137) and experimenting with dippers and sauces that complement each other.

8 cups Chicken Broth (page 137)

2 garlic cloves, crushed

1½ teaspoons kosher salt, plus more for seasoning

2 pounds cubed or sliced raw meats, like pork, chicken, and turkey

3 or 4 additional dippers of your choice

Sauces of your choice

1. In a medium saucepan, bring the broth, garlic, and salt to a simmer over medium heat.
2. Arrange the various dippers and sauces around the pot.
3. Transfer the hot broth to a fondue pot set to medium-high heat.
4. Skewer your chosen item on a fondue fork and place it in the hot broth. Once the item is cooked through, slide it off the fondue fork and onto a plate. Season with salt and sauces.

STORE-BOUGHT SHORTCUT: Butcher shops and gourmet food shops often sell higher-quality store-made broth. Use the best-quality broth you can find for this recipe.

Miso and Lemongrass Broth

SERVES 4 / PREP TIME: 5 MINUTES / **COOK TIME:** 20 MINUTES

If you've ever dined at a Japanese restaurant, you've likely enjoyed a bowl or two of rich, umami-laden miso soup. This recipe calls for the addition of spicy ginger root and refreshing lemongrass for a punch of flavor. You'd never guess this broth is vegan, but it is a smart choice for your vegan and vegetarian guests especially when served with a variety of vegetables and tofu for dipping. It's also a great match for delicate seafood and poultry. Serve with fresh cilantro, lime wedges, and bean sprouts for garnish.

6 cups vegetable broth

2 cups water

½ cup mild yellow miso paste

1 (2-inch) piece fresh ginger, peeled and thickly sliced

1 garlic clove, crushed

2 fresh lemongrass stems, cut into 1-inch-long pieces

1 scallion, white and green parts, cut into 1-inch-long pieces

1 tablespoon soy sauce

1 teaspoon sesame oil

2 pounds cubed or sliced raw meats, like beef, lamb, pork, chicken, turkey, and mixed seafood

3 or 4 additional dippers of your choice

Sauces of your choice

Kosher salt

CONTINUED >

1. In a medium saucepan, whisk the vegetable broth, water, and miso to combine. Add the ginger, garlic, lemongrass, scallion, soy sauce, and sesame oil and bring the broth to a simmer for 15 minutes over medium-high heat.
2. Pass the broth through a fine-mesh strainer to remove the aromatics, and return the broth to the saucepan, bringing to a simmer once more.
3. While the broth simmers, arrange the various dippers and sauces around the fondue pot.
4. Transfer the hot broth to a fondue pot set to medium-high heat.
5. Skewer your chosen item on a fondue fork and place it in the hot broth. Once the item is cooked through, slide it off the fondue fork and onto a plate. Season with salt and sauces.

COOKING TIP: If you need to get dinner on the table in a hurry, prepare the broth, meats, and vegetables the day before. This recipe is perfect for a healthy weeknight meal when time is tight.

Coq Au Vin Fondue

SERVES 4 / PREP TIME: 5 MINUTES / **COOK TIME:** 40 MINUTES

This recipe calls for a mixture of garlic, red wine, and fresh herbs, turning an ordinary chicken broth into one that's rich, luxurious, and aromatic, perfect for dipping French pantry staples. You can enjoy the same flavors of a slow-braised meat stew without the hours spent cooking. Serve with a communal cheese plate for dessert and allow yourself to be transported to the French countryside.

---

2 garlic cloves, crushed

3 shallots, cut into chunks

4 mushrooms, quartered

3 fresh thyme sprigs

2 bay leaves

1 tablespoon extra-virgin olive oil

½ teaspoon whole black peppercorns

1 teaspoon kosher salt, plus more for seasoning

½ cup dry red wine

8 cups chicken broth

2 pounds cubed or sliced raw chicken or turkey

3 or 4 additional dippers of your choice

Sauces of your choice

1. In a saucepan, sauté the garlic, shallots, mushrooms, thyme, and bay leaves in the olive oil over medium-high heat for 3 to 5 minutes, or until the ingredients begin to caramelize.

CONTINUED >

2. Add the peppercorns, salt, wine, and broth, and bring to a simmer over medium-low heat for 35 minutes. Check the broth for seasoning and adjust if necessary.

3. Pass the broth through a fine-mesh strainer, and return to the pot to simmer for 2 to 3 minutes more.

4. While the broth simmers, arrange the various dippers and sauces around the fondue pot.

5. Transfer the hot broth to a fondue pot set to medium-high heat.

6. Skewer your chosen item on a fondue fork and place it in the hot broth. Once the item is cooked through, slide it off the fondue fork and onto a plate. Season with salt and sauces.

SAUCE TIP: Serve with a selection of the following: Mayonnaise (page 126), Roquefort Dip (page 130), Steak Sauce (page 120), Horseradish Cream (page 129), and Dijon or whole-grain mustard.

Mushroom Broth Fondue

SERVES 4 / PREP TIME: 5 MINUTES / **COOK TIME:** 50 MINUTES

Dried mushrooms are the star of the show in this rich and flavorful mushroom broth. When steeped in hot water, dried mushrooms release myriad earthy, meaty, and umami flavors. This full-bodied vegetable-based broth can be a smart choice for the vegan and vegetarian crowd, but it works equally well for cooking your favorite meats.

---

4 cups water

1 cup dried porcini mushrooms

½ small onion, cut into chunks

1 garlic clove, crushed

3 fresh thyme sprigs

1 tablespoon extra-virgin olive oil

4¼ cups vegetable broth

1 tablespoon soy sauce

1 teaspoon sherry vinegar

1 teaspoon kosher salt, plus more for seasoning

½ teaspoon freshly ground black pepper

½ cup cremini mushrooms, thinly sliced

2 pounds cubed or sliced raw meats, like beef, lamb, pork, chicken, turkey, and mixed seafood

2 pounds mixed mushrooms and vegetables (vegan option)

3 or 4 additional dippers of your choice

Sauces of your choice

1. Pour the water into a small pot over medium heat. Add the dried porcini mushrooms and allow the mushrooms to steep in the water like a tea for 10 minutes.

   CONTINUED >

2. In a separate large saucepan, sauté the onion, garlic, and thyme in the olive oil over medium heat for 2 to 3 minutes until the ingredients begin to caramelize. Add the vegetable broth, soy sauce, sherry vinegar, salt, pepper, and mushroom "tea" to the pot, and bring to a simmer over low heat for 30 minutes.

3. Once ready, strain the broth through a fine-mesh strainer, and return the broth to the saucepan, discarding the aromatics.

4. Add the sliced mushrooms to the broth and simmer for 2 to 3 minutes. Check the broth for seasoning and adjust if necessary.

5. While the broth simmers, arrange the various dippers and sauces around the fondue pot.

6. Transfer the hot broth to a fondue pot set to medium-high heat.

7. Skewer your chosen item on a fondue fork and place it in the hot broth. Once the item is cooked through, slide it off the fondue fork onto a plate. Season with salt and sauces.

COOKING TIP: This rich and flavorful broth, along with more sautéed mushrooms, will create the ultimate mushroom risotto. Make extra and freeze them for future use.

Tomato-Saffron Broth Fondue

SERVES 4 / PREP TIME: 5 MINUTES / **COOK TIME:** 30 MINUTES

This recipe takes its cues from the rich seafood stews found along the coast in France and Spain. The unmistakable flavor of saffron shines alongside smoky sweet paprika in this rich, tomato-based broth. Seafood stew is commonly served with Rouille Sauce (page 133)—and a baguette for soaking up all the leftover broth.

---

4 cups water

1 generous pinch Spanish saffron threads

1 garlic clove, minced

2 tablespoons extra-virgin olive oil

2½ cups tomato passata or tomato purée

1 teaspoon kosher salt, plus more for seasoning

¼ teaspoon smoked Spanish paprika

2 pounds raw mixed seafood, like shrimp, scallops, mussels, clams, octopus, calamari, and fin fish

3 or 4 additional dippers of your choice

Sauces of your choice

1. Pour the water into a small pot over medium heat, add the saffron, and allow the saffron to steep in the water like a tea for 10 minutes.
2. In a separate saucepan, sauté the garlic in the olive oil over medium heat for 2 to 3 minutes, stirring regularly to prevent the garlic from burning.
3. Add the tomato passata, salt, paprika, and saffron "tea." Simmer over low heat for 25 to 30 minutes. Check the broth for seasoning and adjust if necessary.

CONTINUED >

4. While the broth simmers, arrange the various dippers and sauces around the fondue pot.

5. Transfer the hot broth to a fondue pot set to medium-high heat.

6. Skewer your chosen item on a fondue fork and place it in the hot broth. Once the item is cooked through, slide it off the fondue fork and onto a plate. Season with salt and sauces.

COOKING TIP: Fresh fish and seafood cook very quickly in hot broth, so pay close attention to ensure your seafood is just cooked through, and not overcooked.

French Onion Broth Fondue

SERVES 4 / PREP TIME: 10 MINUTES / **COOK TIME:** 1 HOUR

A mention of French onion soup is usually followed closely by a chorus of swooning chatter. Everyone loves the combination of slowly caramelized onions and rich, meaty beef broth with a boozy hint of Cognac. Make sure to serve this recipe with lots of baguettes and Gruyère cheese to satisfy all your French onion soup cravings.

---

1 tablespoon salted butter

1 tablespoon extra-virgin olive oil

1 large yellow onion, thinly sliced

4 shallots, peeled and thinly sliced

2 garlic cloves, minced

2 bay leaves

3 fresh thyme sprigs

1½ teaspoons white sugar

1 teaspoon kosher salt, plus more for seasoning

½ teaspoon freshly ground black pepper

1 to 2 tablespoons Cognac or brandy (optional)

½ cup dry white wine

8 cups beef broth

2 pounds cubed or sliced raw meats, like beef, lamb, venison, bison, pork, chicken, and turkey

3 or 4 additional dippers of your choice

Sauces of your choice

CONTINUED >

1. In a medium saucepan, combine the butter, olive oil, onion, shallots, garlic, bay leaves, thyme, sugar, salt, and pepper and sweat over medium-low heat. Stir regularly for 25 to 30 minutes, or until the onions have evenly caramelized. This step is important for developing flavor and cannot be rushed.

2. Add the Cognac (if using), wine, and beef broth. Bring to a simmer over low heat for 30 minutes.

3. Remove and discard the bay leaves and thyme stems. Check the broth for seasoning and adjust if necessary.

4. While the broth simmers, arrange the various dippers and sauces around the fondue pot.

5. Transfer the hot broth to a fondue pot set to medium-high heat.

6. Skewer your chosen item on a fondue fork and place it in the hot broth. Once the item is cooked through, slide it off the fondue fork and onto a plate. Season with additional salt and sauces.

COOKING TIP: Prepare the broth the day before to save preparation time in the kitchen before the meal.

Spicy Szechuan Hot Pot

SERVES 4 / PREP TIME: 5 MINUTES / **COOK TIME:** 40 MINUTES

If you love steaming-hot bowls of spicy broth, this is the Hot Pot dish for you. The Northern Chinese tradition of serving tongue-tingling bowls of boldly seasoned broth with Szechuan peppercorns is the perfect remedy to cold winter days. One way to chase away the spice while keeping the meal authentic is to serve ice-cold Chinese lager to wash it all down.

2 tablespoons peanut oil

3 garlic cloves, crushed

1 (2-inch) piece fresh ginger, peeled and thickly sliced

3 scallions, white and green parts, 2 cut into thirds and 1 thinly sliced

1 tablespoon Szechuan peppercorns

1 cinnamon stick

1 whole star anise

2 bay leaves

3 to 5 dried Chinese red chiles

6¼ cups beef broth

3 cups water

1 to 2 tablespoons fermented red chili bean paste

2 shiitake mushrooms, stemmed and thinly sliced

Kosher salt

2 pounds cubed or sliced raw meats, like beef, lamb, pork, chicken, turkey, and mixed seafood

3 or 4 additional dippers of your choice

Sauces of your choice

CONTINUED >

1. In a medium pot, combine the peanut oil, garlic, ginger, and cut scallions. Sauté over medium-high heat for 3 to 5 minutes, or until the ingredients begin to caramelize.

2. Add the Szechuan peppercorns, cinnamon, star anise, bay leaves, and dried chiles, and continue to sauté for 2 to 3 minutes.

3. Add the beef broth and water, and bring to a simmer. Reduce the heat to medium-low, and simmer for 30 minutes.

4. Strain the broth to remove all the aromatics, and return the broth to the pot.

5. Add the red chili bean paste, mushrooms, and thinly sliced scallions, and return the broth to a simmer for 1 to 2 minutes. Check the broth for seasoning and adjust if necessary.

6. While the broth simmers, arrange the various dippers and sauces around the fondue pot.

7. Transfer the hot broth to a fondue pot set to medium-high heat.

8. Skewer your chosen item on a fondue fork and place it in the hot broth. Once the item is cooked through, slide it off the fondue fork and onto a plate. Season with salt and sauces.

SAUCE TIP: Serve with Korean Gochujang Ketchup (page 134) and Peanut Sauce (page 124) for dipping your meats, dumplings, and vegetables.

Spicy Mexican Broth Fondue

SERVES 4 / PREP TIME: 5 MINUTES / **COOK TIME:** 35 MINUTES

The combination of herbs and spices in this recipe offers a distinctly Mexican flavor. Chili powder and ground cumin give this tomato-based broth a toasty, earthy foundation, and chipotle brings a gentle, smoky heat. Serve this spicy broth with all your favorite Mexican pantry staples to get the fondue fiesta started.

1 garlic clove, minced

¼ cup white onion, minced

1 small jalapeño pepper, stemmed and minced

1 tablespoon extra-virgin olive oil

1 teaspoon chili powder

½ teaspoon ground cumin

1 teaspoon kosher salt, plus more for seasoning

2½ cups tomato passata or tomato purée

4 cups chicken broth

2 whole chipotles in adobo, minced, plus 1 tablespoon adobo sauce

1 teaspoon honey

¼ teaspoon cayenne pepper (optional)

2 pounds cubed or sliced raw meats, like beef, pork, chicken, turkey, and mixed seafood

3 or 4 additional dippers of your choice

Sauces of your choice

CONTINUED >

1. In a medium pot, sauté the garlic, onion, and jalapeño pepper in the olive oil over medium heat for 3 minutes.

2. Add the chili powder, cumin, and salt, and sauté for 2 minutes.

3. Add the passata, broth, chipotles, adobo sauce, honey, and cayenne pepper (if using), and bring to a low simmer for 30 minutes. Check the broth for seasoning and adjust if necessary.

4. While the broth simmers, arrange the various dippers and sauces around the fondue pot.

5. Transfer the hot broth to a fondue pot set to medium-high heat.

6. Skewer your chosen item on a fondue fork and place it in the hot broth. Once the item is cooked through, slide it off the fondue fork and onto a plate. Season with salt and sauces.

SAUCE TIP: Serve with a selection of your favorite salsas, guacamole, and sour cream.

Greek Lemon and Garlic Broth Fondue

SERVES 4 / PREP TIME: 5 MINUTES / **COOK TIME:** 20 MINUTES

This recipe takes its cues from Avgolemono soup, a classic Greek recipe that calls for lots of fresh herbs, lemon, and garlic. The addition of eggs to this broth creates a rich, velvety texture—but be careful not to overheat the broth once the eggs have been added so they won't scramble.

---

2 scallions, white and green parts, thinly sliced

1 large garlic clove, sliced

1 tablespoon extra-virgin olive oil

1 tablespoon fresh oregano leaves, chopped

8⅓ cups chicken broth

1 teaspoon kosher salt, plus more for seasoning

⅓ cup freshly squeezed lemon juice, plus more as needed

2 large eggs

2 pounds cubed or sliced raw meats, like beef, lamb, pork, chicken, turkey, and mixed seafood

3 or 4 additional dippers of your choice

Sauces of your choice

1. In a medium pot, sauté the scallions and garlic in the olive oil over medium-high heat for 3 minutes.
2. Add the oregano, chicken broth, and salt and bring to a simmer for 30 minutes.
3. Pass the broth through a fine-mesh strainer and discard the aromatics.

CONTINUED >

4. Return the broth to the pot and place over medium heat, keeping the broth just below a simmer.

5. In a small bowl, whisk together the lemon juice and eggs. Add ¼ cup of warm broth to the bowl and whisk together to temper the eggs. Add the egg mixture to the pot and whisk to combine. The broth should stay below a simmer to avoid scrambling the eggs. Check the broth for seasoning and adjust if necessary—don't be afraid to add more lemon juice.

6. While the broth simmers, arrange the various dippers and sauces around the fondue pot.

7. Transfer the hot broth to a fondue pot set to medium-high heat.

8. Skewer your chosen item on a fondue fork and place it in the hot broth. Once the item is cooked through, slide it off the fondue fork and onto a plate. Season with salt and sauces.

SAUCE TIP: Serve with Tzatziki Sauce (page 132), olive oil, olives, and Greek pita bread for a well-rounded meal.

CHOCOLATE-ESPRESSO FONDUE (PAGE 109)

6

dessert fondue

DESSERT FONDUE is a great way to celebrate a
special occasion or add a sweet finish to a weeknight meal.
Fresh fruit dippers can turn your dessert fondue into a lighter
treat, or serve cakes and cookie dippers for a more indulgent
experience. You can prepare your dessert fondue
a day or two ahead without compromising quality or flavor,
making it an easy option if tIme is limited.

DELICIOUS DESSERT DIPPERS

Enjoy a decadent dessert fondue experience with dippers like fresh and dried fruits, pretzels, marshmallows, cookies, and cakes. Select a minimum of three or four dippers to end your guests' night on a delicious note. You can use easy store-bought items or more complex options like the homemade shortbread, biscotti, and pound cake recipes found in chapter 7.

- Cubes of Half-Pound Cake (page 147), Angel Food Cake (page 145), fruitcake, gingerbread, brownies, coconut macaroons, waffles, croissants, donut holes, banana bread, cinnamon rolls, scones, and soft pretzels

- Selection of cookies like gingersnaps, stroopwafels, Oreos, wafers, Scottish Shortbread Cookies (page 143), graham crackers, sugar cookies, Almond Biscotti (page 149), and Pirouline brand cookies

- Selection of fresh fruit like grapes, strawberries, bananas, pineapple, apples, pears, and plums

- Pretzels, marshmallows, rice crispy treats, meringues, dried apricots, dried mango, and dried apple slices

Caramel Apple–Brie Fondue

SERVES 4 / PREP TIME: 10 MINUTES / **COOK TIME:** 10 MINUTES

Brie cheese fondue with caramel and apple is a fun addition to your weekend brunch menu. It's not too sweet and pairs well with breakfast favorites like waffles, croissants, and fresh fruit. Kick it up a notch by adding chopped pecans and apple brandy.

---

1 tablespoon salted butter

¼ cup brown sugar

¼ teaspoon ground cinnamon

1 apple, peeled, cored, and diced

8 ounces Brie cheese

½ teaspoon cornstarch

⅓ cup heavy (whipping) cream

1. In a small sauté pan, cook the butter, brown sugar, and cinnamon over medium heat for 3 minutes, or until the butter and sugar come together to form a caramel.
2. Add the apple and cook for 5 minutes, or until the apple is softened and the sauce is thickened. Remove from the heat and set aside.
3. Scrape the bloomy rind off the Brie cheese using the edge of a spoon. Cut the Brie into cubes and place in a bowl. Add the cornstarch and toss to coat.

CONTINUED >

DESSERT FONDUE

4. In a small saucepan, warm the cream over medium heat until very hot but not simmering. Add the Brie a few cubes at a time, stirring as they melt into the cream. Transfer to a fondue pot set to low heat.

5. Spoon the caramel apple topping onto the Brie fondue and serve immediately.

STORE-BOUGHT SHORTCUT: You can substitute a spreadable Brie product for the Brie cubes and omit the cornstarch from the recipe. There are extra stabilizers in this type of product that will encourage the Brie and cream to meld.

Spiked English Custard Fondue

SERVES 4 / PREP TIME: 5 MINUTES / **COOK TIME:** 10 MINUTES

Custard is the perfect partner for cubes of dense Half-Pound Cake (page 147), Crisp Gingersnap Cookies (page 154), and fresh fruit. This classic British sweet cream sauce is thickened with egg yolks, which gives it a rich and velvety texture. This recipe calls for a pinch of warm spices and a splash of whiskey, but the combinations of flavors you can add are endless—try adding chocolate, nuts, or your favorite dessert liqueur.

¾ cup whole milk

½ cup heavy (whipping) cream

½ teaspoon vanilla extract

¼ teaspoon ground cinnamon

¼ teaspoon freshly grated nutmeg

2 tablespoons sugar

2 large egg yolks

1½ teaspoons cornstarch

2 tablespoons whiskey (optional)

1. In a small saucepan, bring the milk, cream, vanilla, cinnamon, and nutmeg to a simmer over medium heat.
2. In a bowl, whisk together the sugar, egg yolks, and cornstarch. Slowly add the hot milk mixture to the egg mixture while whisking constantly.

CONTINUED >

DESSERT FONDUE

3. Return the mixture to the sauce-pan over very low heat and stir continuously until just below a simmer. The custard should thicken enough to coat the back of a wooden spoon. Be careful not to scramble the eggs.

4. Stir in the whiskey (if using) and transfer to a fondue pot set to low heat, or allow to cool completely and refrigerate for up to 2 weeks.

COOKING TIP: The cornstarch is added to this recipe to prevent the sauce from scrambling if it is over-heated in the cooking process. If you notice a grainy texture, pass the sauce through a fine-mesh strainer to remove any scrambled yolk bits.

Salted Caramel Fondue

SERVES 2 / PREP TIME: 5 MINUTES / **COOK TIME:** 10 MINUTES

Salted caramel delivers a big punch of deep caramel flavor everyone will love. The trick is to let the sugar cook until it reaches a medium amber hue, and then add all the butter at once to stop the caramel from darkening any further. Once the butter and cream are emulsified into the sugar, the caramel will develop into a thick consistency perfect for dipping.

---

1 cup white sugar

6 tablespoons (¾ stick) salted butter

⅓ cup heavy (whipping) cream

1 teaspoon kosher salt

1. In a medium saucepan, melt the sugar over medium-low heat, stirring occasionally with a high-heat-resistant rubber spatula or wooden spoon. The sugar will form clumps and eventually melt into a thick, amber-colored liquid as you continue to stir, but keep a close eye on it as it can burn quickly.

2. Once the sugar has completely melted and is a golden amber color, immediately add all the butter. The caramel will bubble rapidly. If the butter separates as you whisk, don't worry. It will still come together.

3. Slowly stir in the cream. Allow the mixture to boil, stirring, for 1 minute. The mixture will rise in the saucepan as it boils.

CONTINUED >

DESSERT FONDUE

4. Remove the saucepan from the heat and stir in the salt. Transfer to a fondue pot set to low heat, or allow to cool completely and refrigerate for up to 1 month.

COOKING TIP: If your sugar burns, there is no way to salvage it. Put the pot in the sink and fill it with hot water to dissolve. Start again with a new pot and fresh sugar—and watch it very closely.

Chocolate Peanut Butter Fondue

SERVES 2 / PREP TIME: 5 MINUTES / **COOK TIME:** 5 MINUTES

Chocolate and peanut butter are a classic combo—and for good reason. This rich and indulgent chocolate fondue is like dipping into a melted peanut butter cup, and almost every sweet treat you can dream up tastes great with this decadent sauce.

½ cup heavy (whipping) cream

¼ cup chunky all-natural
    peanut butter

2 tablespoons sugar

4 ounces semisweet
    chocolate, chopped

½ teaspoon vanilla extract

Pinch kosher salt

1. In a small saucepan, bring the cream, peanut butter, and sugar to just below a simmer over medium heat and remove from the heat.
2. Stir in the chocolate, vanilla, and salt until the chocolate is melted and the sauce has a smooth consistency. If needed, place the saucepan back over low heat.
3. Transfer to a fondue pot set to low heat, or allow to cool completely and refrigerate for up to 2 weeks.

STORE-BOUGHT SHORTCUT: There are endless chocolate sauce and fondue options available for purchase. Look for best-quality options that list chocolate as a main ingredient. Add a tablespoon or two of your favorite all-natural peanut butter to the chocolate as you warm it up for similar results.

Chocolate Crème Fraîche Fondue

SERVES 2 / PREP TIME: 5 MINUTES / **COOK TIME:** 5 MINUTES

This recipe combines the nutty flavors of semisweet dark chocolate with the creamy tang of crème fraîche. Together, they form a rich and decadent chocolate sauce with a smooth and luxurious texture that begs to be enjoyed with fresh fruit like strawberries and pineapple.

¼ cup crème fraîche

¼ cup heavy (whipping) cream

1 tablespoon white sugar

6 ounces semisweet chocolate, chopped

1. In a small saucepan, combine the crème fraîche, cream, and sugar over medium heat. Bring to just below a simmer then remove from the heat.
2. Stir in the chocolate until it melts completely and the sauce has a smooth consistency. If needed, place the saucepan back over low heat.
3. Transfer to a fondue pot set to low heat, or allow to cool completely and refrigerate for up to 2 weeks.

COOKING TIP: If you can't find (or make) crème fraîche, you can substitute sour cream or plain full-fat Greek yogurt for a similar effect.

Chocolate-Espresso Fondue

SERVES 2 / PREP TIME: 10 MINUTES / **COOK TIME:** 5 MINUTES

People who love chocolate tend to be equally enthusiastic about coffee—and when you put them together, the magic happens. I recommend using high-quality chocolate as a match for the nutty, smoky flavors that coffee adds to this combination. You can take this grown-up indulgence to another level with the addition of your favorite liqueur, too. Try Kahlua, Frangelico, or Irish Cream, to name a few.

¼ cup hot water

1 tablespoon instant espresso

2 tablespoons liqueur (optional)

¼ cup heavy (whipping) cream

1 teaspoon sugar

6 ounces semisweet
    chocolate, chopped

1. In a bowl, mix together the hot water and instant espresso and set aside for 5 minutes. Add the liqueur (if using).
2. In a small saucepan, bring the prepared espresso, heavy cream, and sugar to just below a simmer over low heat.
3. Stir in the chocolate until it melts completely and the sauce has a smooth consistency. If needed, return the saucepan to low heat.
4. Transfer to a fondue pot set to low heat, or allow to cool completely and refrigerate for up to 2 weeks.

COOKING TIP: Percolator coffee is a good replacement for instant espresso. Take ½ cup of coffee and bring it to a simmer to reduce to ¼ cup of liquid.

DESSERT FONDUE

Bourbon-Butterscotch Fondue

SERVES 2 / PREP TIME: 5 MINUTES / **COOK TIME:** 5 MINUTES

The primary ingredients in homemade butterscotch are brown sugar, butter, and cream, which together produce a sauce with a toffee-like flavor. This recipe calls for the addition of bourbon, which is the perfect boozy match to this sweet and creamy sauce. If you have any left over, it's absolutely delicious spooned over vanilla ice cream.

3 tablespoons dark brown sugar

2 tablespoons white sugar

½ cup corn syrup

2 tablespoons salted butter

½ cup heavy (whipping) cream

2 tablespoons bourbon

1. Put the brown sugar, white sugar, corn syrup, and butter in a medium saucepan over medium heat, and stir to combine. Bring to a boil and cook for 5 minutes, stirring a couple times.
2. Add the cream and bourbon and stir together. Boil for 1 minute.
3. Transfer to a fondue pot set to low heat, or allow to cool completely and refrigerate for up to 1 month.

COOKING TIP: This recipe makes for a great gift for the foodie in your life. Make a double or triple batch and divide into glass jars for easy gifting.

Cheesecake Fondue

SERVES 2 / PREP TIME: 5 MINUTES / **COOK TIME:** 5 MINUTES

If you love cheesecake, this recipe is for you. Served warm or cold, this rich and creamy sauce is delicious with a selection of your favorite fruits and dippers, like fresh strawberries and vanilla pound cake. Toasted pistachios or almonds make for a great addition to this simple recipe.

½ cup heavy (whipping) cream

¼ cup crème fraîche

¼ cup mascarpone cheese

½ cup cream cheese

2 teaspoons sugar

½ teaspoon vanilla extract

⅛ teaspoon ground cinnamon

¼ cup white chocolate chips

1. In a small saucepan, combine the cream, crème fraîche, mascarpone, cream cheese, sugar, vanilla, and cinnamon. Bring to just below a simmer over low heat, stirring until you get a smooth consistency. Remove from the heat.
2. Add the white chocolate chips and stir to combine. Make sure all the chocolate is melted, and transfer to a fondue pot set to low heat, or allow to cool completely and refrigerate for up to 1 week.

COOKING TIP: Make sure all ingredients are at room temperature before cooking for a faster, more consistent experience.

White Chocolate–Marshmallow Fondue

SERVES 2 / PREP TIME: 5 MINUTES / **COOK TIME:** 5 MINUTES

If you love s'mores, you will enjoy this oozy marshmallow fondue. This recipe can be made with milk or dark chocolate chips instead of the white chocolate, if you prefer. Use graham crackers as a dipper for the complete s'mores experience.

¼ cup heavy (whipping) cream

1 tablespoon salted butter

½ cup mini marshmallows, packed

½ cup white chocolate chips

1. In a small saucepan, melt the cream, butter, and marshmallows over low heat, heating the mixture just enough to be quite warm but not at a simmer. Remove from the heat.
2. Add the white chocolate chips and stir to combine until all the chocolate is melted. Return to low heat if necessary.
3. Transfer to a fondue pot set to low heat, or allow to cool completely and refrigerate for up to 1 week.

STORE-BOUGHT SHORTCUT: Marshmallow fondue is not available for purchase, but you can melt together chocolate sauce and marshmallow fluff for a similar option.

Maple Cream Fondue

SERVES 2 / PREP TIME: 5 MINUTES / **COOK TIME:** 5 MINUTES

Maple cream is so simple to make and awesome as a topping for French toast, crepes, and waffles. I recommend adding it to your regular brunch repertoire. Serve this classic Canadian indulgence with dippers like cubes of croissant, apple slices, and shortbread cookies.

½ cup pure maple syrup

1 tablespoon cold water

1 tablespoon cornstarch

½ cup heavy (whipping) cream

Pinch kosher salt

1. In a small saucepan, bring the maple syrup to a simmer over medium heat.
2. In a small bowl, combine the water and cornstarch.
3. Add the cornstarch slurry, cream, and salt to the saucepan and whisk to combine. Bring to a full simmer for 1 minute and remove from the heat.
4. Transfer to a fondue pot set to low heat, or allow to cool completely and refrigerate for up to 1 week.

COOKING TIP: Maple-flavored table syrup is not a recommended replacement for pure maple syrup. However, maple extract could be added to the Spiked English Custard Fondue recipe (page 103) for a similar dessert.

Vegan Toasted Coconut Fondue

SERVES 2 / PREP TIME: 5 MINUTES / **COOK TIME:** 5 MINUTES

This coconut milk custard combines toasted coconut, vanilla, and cinnamon, and it happens to be vegan. This custard is every bit as luxurious as one made with eggs and dairy. Serve alongside your favorite selection of fruits, vegan cookies, and vegan cakes for dunking.

¼ cup sweetened coconut flakes

1½ cups coconut milk
(1 [13.5 ounce] can)

¼ cup white sugar

1½ teaspoons cornstarch

½ teaspoon vanilla extract

¼ teaspoon ground cinnamon

1. Preheat the oven to 350°F and line a baking sheet with parchment paper.
2. Put the coconut on the prepared baking sheet and toast in the oven for 2 to 3 minutes, or until golden brown. Watch closely because the coconut can burn quickly.
3. In a small saucepan, whisk together the milk, sugar, cornstarch, vanilla, and cinnamon until well combined. Bring to a full simmer over medium heat, stirring often. Remove from the heat once the mixture is thickened.
4. Add the toasted coconut to the custard and stir to combine.
5. Transfer to a fondue pot set to low heat, or allow to cool completely and refrigerate for up to 1 week.

COOKING TIP: You can toast the coconut in a nonstick pan on the stovetop over medium-low heat. Stir with a nonstick heat-resistant spatula and watch closely to avoid burning.

Bananas Foster Fondue

SERVES 2 / PREP TIME: 10 MINUTES / **COOK TIME:** 10 MINUTES

The classic Bananas Foster recipe originated in New Orleans in the 1950s. In this fondue, all the same great flavors of butter, banana, and dark rum are turned into a sauce for dunking your favorite dessert fondue dippers. Over-ripe bananas will become mushy when sautéed, so choose a banana that is just starting to ripen for this recipe.

---

1 cup white sugar

7 tablespoons salted butter, divided

⅓ cup heavy (whipping) cream

1 banana, peeled and diced

1 tablespoon brown sugar

½ teaspoon ground cinnamon

2 tablespoons dark rum

2 tablespoons banana liqueur (optional)

1. In a medium saucepan, melt the white sugar over medium-low heat, stirring occasionally with a high-heat-resistant rubber spatula or wooden spoon. The sugar will form clumps and eventually melt into a thick, amber-colored liquid as you continue to stir. But keep a close eye on it because it can burn quickly.

2. Once the sugar has completely melted and is a golden amber color, immediately add 6 tablespoons of butter. The caramel will bubble rapidly, and if the butter separates a bit as you whisk, don't worry. It will still come together.

CONTINUED >

3. Slowly stir in the cream. The mixture will bubble, but keep stirring. Boil for 1 minute. The mixture will rise as you stir it in the pan. Remove from the heat and set aside.

4. In a small sauté pan, combine the remaining 1 tablespoon of butter, the banana, the brown sugar, and the cinnamon, and sauté over high heat for 2 minutes, or until everything starts to melt together. Add the rum and banana liqueur (if using) and sauté for 1 to 2 minutes. Add this mixture to the caramel sauce and stir to combine.

5. Transfer to a fondue pot set to low heat, or allow to cool completely and refrigerate for up to 1 week.

STORE-BOUGHT SHORTCUT: You can make this recipe by substituting with best-quality store-bought caramel sauce. Jump ahead to step 4 in this recipe and add the sautéed bananas to the caramel sauce for a similar dish.

7

dippers & sauces

YOUR FONDUE experience isn't complete until you
have chosen the perfect list of dippers and sauces
to accompany the meal. Typically, you should serve two to
three sauces and three to four dippers with fondue.
Many store-bought options are available to help save you time in the
kitchen, but there is nothing quite like homemade cookies,
cakes, and sauces. Many of these recipes can be
prepared a day or two ahead, or made in batches
and frozen for future use.

Steak Sauce

SERVES 4 / PREP TIME: 10 MINUTES / **COOK TIME:** 30 MINUTES

Steak sauce, sometimes referred to as brown sauce or HP sauce, is served with everything from Sunday roast to fried egg and bacon sandwiches. Yes, there are a lot of ingredients, but they produce a sauce with many layers of flavor.

---

1 cup seeded and diced tomato

½ cup peeled, cored, and diced apple

¼ cup minced shallot

1 garlic clove, minced

1 (1-inch) piece ginger, peeled and minced

1 teaspoon extra-virgin olive oil

4 dates, pitted and diced

1½ cups water

2 teaspoons tomato paste

¼ cup brown sugar

1 tablespoon molasses

1 tablespoon Worcestershire sauce

¼ cup red-wine vinegar

5 whole juniper berries, crushed

¼ teaspoon ground star anise

⅛ teaspoon ground cloves

¼ teaspoon whole mustard seeds

⅛ teaspoon ground allspice

1 teaspoon kosher salt

½ teaspoon freshly ground black pepper

1. In a medium pot, sweat the tomato, apple, shallot, garlic, and ginger in the olive oil over medium heat for 5 minutes.
2. Add the dates, water, tomato paste, brown sugar, molasses, Worcestershire sauce, vinegar, juniper berries, star anise, cloves, mustard seeds, allspice, salt, and pepper, and bring to a simmer. Reduce the heat to low and simmer uncovered, stirring occasionally, for about 25 minutes, or until it has a sauce-like consistency.
3. Puree with a handheld emulsion or countertop blender.
4. Pass the sauce through a medium-mesh strainer and allow to cool completely.
5. Store the sauce in the refrigerator for up to 2 weeks.

COOKING TIP: If the sauce is too thin once blended, return it to the pot and continue to simmer to get the desired consistency.

Béarnaise Sauce

SERVES 4 / PREP TIME: 5 MINUTES / **COOK TIME:** 15 MINUTES

Béarnaise sauce is a grown-up Hollandaise sauce—a luxurious emulsion of vinegar reduction, butter, egg yolks, and fresh tarragon. This sauce is so delicious, you will rarely have leftovers, and that's a good thing, since it does not keep well in the refrigerator.

¼ cup white-wine vinegar

1 small shallot, peeled and minced

½ teaspoon crushed black pepper

1 tablespoon fresh tarragon leaves, plus 1 teaspoon, divided

1 tablespoon water

2 large egg yolks

12 tablespoons (1½ sticks) unsalted butter, melted

Kosher salt

Freshly squeezed lemon juice

1. In a small saucepan, combine the vinegar, shallot, pepper, and 1 tablespoon of tarragon. Bring to a simmer over medium heat, and cook for about 5 minutes to reduce by half. Remove from the heat, and let cool.
2. Put the cooled shallot and tarragon mixture in a small stainless steel mixing bowl along with the water and egg yolks, and whisk to combine.
3. Put 2 inches of water in a small saucepan and bring to a boil, then reduce the heat to the lowest setting. Place the bowl on top of the saucepan, making sure that it does not touch the water directly. Whisk the yolk mixture until it thickens, for 5 to 7 minutes. The volume should double.

4. Slowly whisk in the butter until it has emulsified into the yolks. Season with salt and lemon juice. If the sauce is too thick, stir in a splash of hot water.
5. Add the remaining 1 teaspoon of tarragon, and serve immediately.

DIPPERS: Serve Béarnaise sauce with poultry and fish dishes or pork and red meats.

Peanut Sauce

SERVES 4 / PREP TIME: 5 MINUTES

This recipe for peanut sauce pulls together all the traditional flavors of the Asian pantry—fresh garlic, ginger, and bird's-eye chiles—in less than 5 minutes. Tofu is a great match for this flavorful sauce, though it's also delicious with other proteins like poultry, fish, and grilled red meats.

½ cup chunky natural peanut butter

3 tablespoons soy sauce

¼ cup coconut milk, plus more as needed

2 tablespoons rice vinegar

3 tablespoons brown sugar

1 garlic clove, minced

1 (1-inch) piece ginger, peeled and minced

1 small bird's-eye chile pepper, stemmed and thinly sliced (optional)

1. In a medium bowl, whisk together the peanut butter, soy sauce, coconut milk, vinegar, brown sugar, garlic, ginger, and chile pepper (if using).
2. Thin out with a splash more coconut milk or water, if the sauce is too thick.
3. Keep refrigerated for up to 2 weeks.

SAUCE TIP: Use this sauce for dressing Asian noodle salads, chicken satay skewers, and fresh spring rolls.

Tartar Sauce

SERVES 4 / PREP TIME: 5 MINUTES

Tartar sauce is most commonly served as a creamy condiment for fried fish, and this homemade recipe offers a lighter, more refreshing option for all types of seafood and poultry. Serve this with any of the Bourguignonne or broth fondue recipes that use fish and poultry dippers.

⅔ cup mayonnaise

¼ cup sour cream

2 teaspoons white-wine vinegar

1 teaspoon capers, finely chopped

1 teaspoon finely chopped cornichon pickle

1 teaspoon finely chopped sweet pickle

1 teaspoon fresh dill, finely chopped

¼ teaspoon freshly ground black pepper

1. In a small bowl, using a spatula, mix together the mayonnaise, sour cream, vinegar, capers, cornichon pickles, sweet pickles, dill, and pepper until fully combined.
2. Keep this sauce refrigerated until ready to serve, for up to 1 week.

COOKING TIP: The addition of sour cream and fresh herbs makes this home-made recipe lighter and more refreshing than store-bought versions. Use the highest-quality mayonnaise you can find, or make a homemade version.

DIPPERS & SAUCES

Mayonnaise

SERVES 4 / PREP TIME: 5 MINUTES / **COOK TIME:** 5 MINUTES

Homemade mayonnaise offers a richness the store-bought versions can't deliver. Use this recipe as a foundation for other recipes in this chapter, like Tartar Sauce (page 125), Curry Aioli (page 128), and Roquefort Dip (page 130), or use it as a condiment.

---

1 large egg, at room temperature

1 tablespoon Dijon mustard

1 tablespoon red-wine vinegar

¼ teaspoon Kosher salt, plus more for seasoning

1 cup canola oil, plus more as needed

1 teaspoon freshly squeezed lemon juice or vinegar

1. Put the egg in a food processor and process for 20 seconds. Add the mustard, vinegar, and salt and blend for another 20 seconds.
2. Scrape the sides and bottom with a spatula, turn the food processor on, and begin to add the oil a few drops at a time until about ¼ cup has been added. This step should take 2 to 3 minutes and is crucial to emulsifying the mayonnaise.
3. Once the mayonnaise starts to thicken, slowly add the rest of the oil in a thin, steady stream.

4. Scrape the sides and bottom with a spatula and process for 10 seconds. Taste the mayonnaise for seasoning and add salt and lemon juice to taste.
5. If the mayonnaise is emulsified but too thin, turn the processor on and slowly stream in more oil, until thick. Check the seasoning again and adjust if necessary.
6. Refrigerate the mayonnaise until ready to serve.

COOKING TIP: Adding the oil in a slow and steady stream helps ensure your mayonnaise doesn't break. If it does, add ½ teaspoon of Dijon mustard to a separate bowl, and slowly whisk the broken mayonnaise into the mustard.

Curry Aioli

SERVES 2 / PREP TIME: 5 MINUTES

Aioli is basically mayonnaise with added garlic and other seasonings. This recipe calls for curry powder, an aromatic blend of spices like coriander, cumin, cardamom, ginger, and turmeric commonly found in Indian cuisine. Serve this flavorful aioli with Classic Beef Broth Hot Pot (page 79), Classic Chicken Broth Hot Pot (page 80), and Indian Masala Fondue (page 36).

¼ cup good-quality mayonnaise

¼ cup crème fraîche or sour cream

1 tablespoon curry powder

1½ teaspoons freshly squeezed lemon juice

½ teaspoon honey

⅛ teaspoon cayenne powder

¼ teaspoon kosher salt, plus more for seasoning

1. In a small bowl, whisk together the mayonnaise, crème fraîche, curry powder, lemon juice, honey, cayenne powder, and salt to form an emulsified aioli.
2. Taste the sauce and adjust the seasonings.
3. Refrigerate the aioli until ready to serve, for up to 2 weeks.

COOKING TIP: The flavors in this aioli intensify as the aioli rests in the refrigerator. Make this recipe a day or two ahead to save time and allow the flavors to bloom.

Horseradish Cream

SERVES 4 / PREP TIME: 5 MINUTES

Horseradish is a root vegetable used as a spice for condiments and cocktails. When mixed with cream, it becomes perfect for serving alongside thick slabs of roasted prime rib of beef, with rich beef gravy and Yorkshire puddings for sopping it all up. I recommend using fresh horseradish for a pure flavor experience, but it can be hard to find. Prepared horseradish also works; just make sure to drain the excess vinegar it is preserved in.

---

1 cup full-fat sour cream

1 teaspoon Dijon mustard

1 teaspoon Worcestershire sauce

1 teaspoon white-wine vinegar

¼ cup finely grated fresh horseradish

½ teaspoon kosher salt, plus more for seasoning

¼ teaspoon freshly ground black pepper, plus more for seasoning

1. In a small bowl, whisk together the sour cream, mustard, Worcestershire sauce, vinegar, horseradish, salt, and black pepper.
2. Taste the sauce and adjust the seasonings.
3. Refrigerate until you are ready to serve, for up to 1 week.

COOKING TIP: Look for fresh horseradish in the produce section of your local grocery store.

Roquefort Dip

SERVES 4 / PREP TIME: 5 MINUTES

Roquefort is a full-bodied sheep's milk blue cheese that packs a hefty punch of salty blue flavor. If you prefer, choose a medium-strength blue cheese like Stilton or Buttermilk Blue. The combination of mayonnaise and crème fraîche builds a creamy foundation for this sauce and allows all the intricate blue cheese notes to shine. Serve this condiment with red meats and poultry.

½ cup good-quality mayonnaise

¼ cup crème fraîche or sour cream

½ cup crumbled Roquefort cheese

1 teaspoon freshly squeezed
   lemon juice

1 garlic clove, minced (optional)

1 tablespoon finely chopped
   fresh chives

¼ teaspoon freshly ground black
   pepper, plus more for seasoning

1. Put the mayonnaise, crème fraîche, Roquefort, lemon juice, garlic (if using), chives, and pepper in a bowl and gently mix with a spatula to combine. Be careful not to break up the cheese crumbles.
2. Taste the sauce and adjust the seasonings.
3. Refrigerate until you are ready to serve, for up to 1 week.

COOKING TIP: Leftover Roquefort sauce can be used as a flavorful addition to sandwiches and salads, and as a dip for Buffalo-style chicken wings.

Vietnamese Nuoc Cham Sauce

SERVES 4 / PREP TIME: 5 MINUTES

Nuoc Cham has an important role in Vietnamese food; crisp-fried spring rolls are dipped into this flavor-packed sauce that combines the four pillars of Vietnamese cuisine—sweet, sour, salty, and spicy. Use this light dipping sauce for anything from seafood to tempura-battered vegetables and grilled meats.

½ cup warm water

¼ cup white sugar

¼ cup freshly squeezed lime juice

2 tablespoons fish sauce

1 tablespoon rice vinegar

1 garlic clove, minced

1 (1-inch) piece ginger, peeled and minced

½ to 1 bird's-eye chile pepper, thinly sliced (optional)

1. In a small bowl, whisk together the water, sugar, lime juice, fish sauce, vinegar, garlic, ginger, and chile pepper (if using).
2. Taste the sauce and adjust the seasonings.
3. Refrigerate until you are ready to serve, for up to 1 week.

COOKING TIP: Nuoc Cham is a great marinade for grilled meats like beef, pork, and chicken. Marinate for 3 to 4 hours before grilling.

Tzatziki Sauce

SERVES 4 / PREP TIME: 5 MINUTES

A trip to your favorite Greek restaurant is never complete until a platter of fresh pita bread and tangy, garlicky tzatziki sauce appears. The combination of lemon, garlic, fresh dill, and cucumber is a refreshing partner for fish, poultry, and grilled meats like lamb and pork.

¾ cup Greek yogurt

½ cup grated cucumber, pressed dry

2 teaspoons freshly squeezed
  lemon juice

1 tablespoon extra-virgin olive oil

1 tablespoon fresh dill,
  finely chopped

1 garlic clove, minced

½ teaspoon kosher salt, plus more
  for seasoning

1. In a small bowl, stir together the yogurt, cucumber, lemon juice, olive oil, dill, garlic, and salt.
2. Taste the sauce and adjust the seasonings.
3. Refrigerate until you are ready to serve, for up to 1 week.

COOKING TIP: If your cucumber is particularly juicy, use cheesecloth or a fine-mesh strainer to help wring out the juices. Excess liquid will make this sauce runny.

Rouille Sauce

SERVES 4 / PREP TIME: 5 MINUTES / COOK TIME: 10 MINUTES

Rouille is an amped-up version of homemade mayonnaise that features roasted red pepper, garlic, and saffron. Slather this thick sauce on grilled slices of baguette and soak up the broth at the bottom of your seafood stew for a luxurious taste of the Mediterranean.

½ roasted red bell pepper, peeled and seeded

1 large egg yolk

1 teaspoon freshly squeezed lemon juice

1 small pinch saffron threads

1 clove garlic, chopped

½ cup vegetable oil

½ cup extra-virgin olive oil

Kosher salt

Freshly ground black pepper

1. In a food processor, combine the red pepper, egg yolk, lemon juice, saffron, and garlic, and pulse until smooth.
2. In a small bowl, mix together the vegetable oil and olive oil. Slowly add the oils in a thin, continuous stream to the food processor until the mixture thickens to a mayonnaise-like consistency.
3. Season with salt and pepper.
4. Serve immediately, or refrigerate for up to 1 week.

COOKING TIP: In a pinch, you can substitute jarred roasted red peppers for this recipe. Make sure to dry the pepper to remove any excess oil or pickling liquid before you add it to the other ingredients.

Korean Gochujang Ketchup

SERVES 4 / PREP TIME: 5 MINUTES

Gochujang is a Korean red chili paste that combines the sweet-and-salty flavors of Korean red chiles, glutinous rice, and meju, a fermented soybean powder. If you like kimchi, then you will enjoy the rich, fermented umami flavors of gochujang. Ketchup and brown sugar sweeten this condiment, and the remaining ingredients add a savory balance. Use this sauce as a garnish for seafood, poultry, and red meats or as a punch of flavor for vegetarian and vegan cuisine.

½ cup ketchup

2 tablespoons Korean red chili paste (gochujang)

2 tablespoons brown sugar

1 tablespoon soy sauce

1 teaspoon hoisin sauce

½ teaspoon sesame oil

1 garlic clove, minced

1 (1-inch) piece ginger, peeled and minced

1. In a small bowl, whisk together the ketchup, chili paste, brown sugar, soy sauce, hoisin sauce, sesame oil, garlic, and ginger.
2. Taste the sauce and adjust the seasonings.
3. Refrigerate until you are ready to serve, for up to 2 weeks.

SAUCE TIP: Use this condiment to add a Korean twist to roasted chicken wings or as a dip for spring rolls and French fries.

Classic Beef Broth

SERVES 4 (10 CUPS) / PREP TIME: 5 MINUTES / **COOK TIME:** 3 HOURS

Beef broth is a foundation for countless soup and sauce recipes, making it an important ingredient for every home cook. Make an extra batch to freeze so you always have homemade beef broth on hand.

---

5 pounds meaty beef bones

2 medium carrots, peeled and cut into 2-inch pieces

2 celery stalks, peeled and cut into 2-inch pieces

2 medium yellow onions, quartered

2 tablespoons tomato paste

2 bay leaves

3 fresh thyme sprigs

3 fresh parsley sprigs

1 tablespoon whole black peppercorns

6 quarts water

1. Preheat the oven to 425°F. On the middle rack, put the bones on a rimmed baking sheet and roast until browned, for about 25 minutes.
2. In a medium mixing bowl, toss the carrots, celery, and onions with the tomato paste. Add to the bones and roast for 25 minutes.
3. Transfer the roasted bones and vegetables to a stockpot, leaving behind any excess rendered fat. Add the bay leaves, thyme, parsley, peppercorns, and water. Slowly bring to a boil over medium heat then reduce to

CONTINUED >

low and simmer, uncovered, for about 3 hours. Periodically skim the surface to remove impurities that float up. The broth is finished when it has reduced to the level of the bones.

4. Strain the broth through a fine-mesh strainer into a large container, cover, and refrigerate for up to 5 days. The broth can be frozen for up to 3 months once it is chilled.

COOKING TIP: You can skip the step of roasting the bones and vegetables, but the broth will be much lighter in color and flavor. Instead, increase the length of cooking time so the broth will reduce and concentrate.

Chicken Broth

SERVES 4 (10 CUPS) / PREP TIME: 5 MINUTES / COOK TIME: 1 HOUR 30 MINUTES

Like beef broth, chicken broth offers an abundance of nutrient-dense richness and depth of flavor that simply cannot be found in store-bought versions. Homemade chicken broth adds quality and character to all your home cooking. By saving chicken bones from whole roasted chickens, you can make broth that will cost almost nothing from the leftovers.

---

2 pounds meaty chicken bones

1 garlic clove, peeled

2 celery stalks, peeled and cut into 1-inch pieces

2 carrots, cut into 1-inch pieces

1 onion, quartered

2 bay leaves

3 parsley sprigs

½ teaspoon kosher salt

1 teaspoon whole black peppercorns

12 cups cold water

1. Put the bones, garlic, celery, carrots, onion, bay leaves, parsley, salt, peppercorns, and water in a large pot. Bring to a rolling boil and reduce the heat to medium-low.
2. Simmer for about 90 minutes, and periodically skim the surface to remove impurities that float up.
3. Strain the broth through a fine-mesh strainer, and cover and refrigerate for up to 5 days. Or, freeze for up to 3 months.

COOKING TIP: Add cleaned leftover trimmings of other vegetables like zucchini, mushrooms, and peppers to add more character to your broth.

DIPPERS & SAUCES

Grilled Vegetables

SERVES 6 / PREP TIME: 15 MINUTES / **COOK TIME:** 25 MINUTES

Grilled vegetables are a simple way to lighten up any savory fondue recipe. Perfect veggies are properly seasoned and cooked through but not mushy. Cut them thick enough to hold their shape as you skewer them for dipping into hot pots of broth and cheese fondue.

⅓ cup extra-virgin olive oil

1 garlic clove, minced

3 red, yellow, or orange bell peppers, halved and seeded

3 green zucchini, cut lengthwise into ½-inch-thick slices

3 yellow squash, cut lengthwise into ½-inch-thick slices

12 cremini mushrooms, stems trimmed

1 Japanese eggplant, cut lengthwise into ½-inch-thick slices

1 bunch asparagus, stems trimmed

½ teaspoon kosher salt

½ teaspoon freshly ground black pepper

1. Place a cast-iron grill pan over medium-high heat or prepare a grill on medium-high heat.
2. In a bowl, mix together the olive oil and garlic. Put the peppers, zucchini, squash, mushrooms, eggplant, and asparagus on a baking sheet and brush evenly with the olive oil mixture. Sprinkle with the salt and pepper.

3. Working in batches, grill the vegetables on both sides until they are lightly charred all over. The goal is to cook each vegetable until they are just tender: Keep in mind, these vegetables will finish cooking in the fondue pot. Each vegetable will take anywhere from 6 to 8 minutes to cook, depending on the thickness.
4. Cut the vegetables into bite-size pieces, big enough to skewer on a fondue fork. Serve warm.

STORE-BOUGHT SHORTCUT: Precut vegetables are an easy way to save some preparation time. Prepare the olive oil and garlic mixture and toss them to coat, season with salt and pepper, then complete the recipe by cooking the vegetables on a grill until tender and lightly charred.

Steamed Vegetables

SERVES 6 / PREP TIME: 15 MINUTES **/ COOK TIME:** 10 MINUTES

Crisp-steamed vegetables are a healthy addition to savory fondues. Use this recipe to prepare the perfect steamed vegetable: not too soft, not too hard, and properly seasoned. The most important step is to cut vegetables uniform in size for even steaming.

---

12 mini potatoes, halved

12 Brussels sprouts, halved with stems and outer leaves removed

2 carrots, peeled and cut into ½-inch slices

½ broccoli crown, cut into bite-size florets

½ cauliflower head, cut into bite-size florets

⅓ cup unsalted butter, melted

2 tablespoons freshly squeezed lemon juice

Kosher salt

Freshly ground black pepper

1. Using a medium pot and steamer basket, add water to just below the steamer basket. Bring the water to a rolling boil and reduce the heat to a simmer.
2. Add the mini potatoes to the basket and steam for 5 minutes.
3. Add the Brussels sprouts, carrots, broccoli, and cauliflower and steam for another 5 to 6 minutes.
4. In a bowl, mix together the melted butter and lemon juice.

5. Transfer the vegetables to a mixing bowl, gently toss with the butter mixture, and sprinkle with salt and pepper to taste. Serve immediately.

COOKING TIP: Use the end of a sharp paring knife inserted into the thickest part of the vegetable to test doneness. The goal is to cook each vegetable until just tender but not mushy. Keep in mind that these vegetables will finish cooking in the fondue pot.

Tempura Batter

SERVES 4 / PREP TIME: 10 MINUTES, PLUS 15 MINUTES TO CHILL

Tempura batter gives a thin, crispy batter coating to anything from bites of fish and seafood to vegetables and even sweets like cubes of cake and cookies. It is important to keep all the ingredients very cold so that when the batter hits the hot oil, it puffs into a light and crispy coating. Make a fresh batch of batter if you plan to fry both savory and sweet dippers over the course of your fondue.

---

1 large egg
¾ cup ice-cold water

1 cup all-purpose flour

1. Using a fork or chopsticks, in a bowl, mix together the egg and cold water until all the egg white is combined with the yolk.
2. Add the flour and mix until just combined—a few small lumps of flour are okay.
3. Chill in the refrigerator for at least 15 minutes before using.

COOKING TIP: Gently coat each item to be fried in cornstarch and shake off any excess. Keep your oil temperature between 340°F and 350°F for a light, crispy tempura.

Scottish Shortbread Cookies

SERVES 6 / PREP TIME: 15 MINUTES / **COOK TIME:** 15 MINUTES

The addition of brown sugar gives these traditional shortbread cookies a rich and caramelized flavor common to Scottish baking. The salted butter in this recipe balances out the sweetness with just a tiny hint of salt. These buttery cookies are perfect for dunking in pots of warmed chocolate, custard, and caramel.

1 cup (2 sticks) salted butter, at room temperature

½ cup brown sugar

2 cups all-purpose flour, plus more for dusting

1. Preheat the oven to 350°F. Line 2 baking sheets with parchment paper.
2. Using a mixer, cream together the butter and sugar until light and fluffy, for about 2 minutes.
3. Add the flour and mix well to combine.
4. Turn the dough out onto a lightly floured work surface, and knead the dough for 4 to 5 minutes to form a soft dough.
5. Roll out the dough into a ½-inch-thick rectangle. Using a knife or pizza cutter, cut into 3-by-1-inch cookies.

CONTINUED >

6. Transfer the cookies to the prepared baking sheets, placing them 1 inch apart. Prick the cookies with a fork and bake until they are lightly browned, for 12 to 15 minutes, rotating the sheets once about halfway through.

7. Transfer the baked cookies to a cooling rack and allow to cool before serving.

STORE-BOUGHT SHORTCUT: There is no end to shortbread cookies available for purchase, but not all of them are created equal. Look for cookies that list butter as the first or second ingredient.

Angel Food Cake

SERVES 4 / PREP TIME: 20 MINUTES / **COOK TIME:** 40 MINUTES

Feathery-light angel food cake is a great addition to any sweet fondue experience. Cut it into cubes and dunk it into any number of dessert flavors. Once baked, properly covered angel food cake keeps for 5 days in the refrigerator and can be frozen for up to 3 months.

1¾ cups white sugar

1 cup plus 2 tablespoons cake flour

¼ teaspoon kosher salt

12 large egg whites, at room temperature

1½ teaspoons cream of tartar

1½ teaspoons vanilla extract

1. Position a rack in the center of the oven and preheat to 350°F.
2. In a food processor, blend the sugar until it is fine and powdery, for about 2 minutes. Remove 1 cup of sugar and set aside. Add the cake flour and salt to the food processor and blend to combine. Separate into 3 equal parts and set aside.
3. In a stand mixer fitted with a whisk attachment, or with a hand mixer and a medium mixing bowl, whip the egg whites and cream of tartar on medium-low speed until foamy, for about 1 minute.

CONTINUED >

4. Increase the speed to medium-high, and slowly add the 1 cup of processed sugar. Whip until soft peaks form, for 5 to 6 minutes. Add the vanilla and whip to combine.

5. Sift one part of the flour mixture into the egg white mixture using a fine-mesh strainer, and gently fold it in with a rubber spatula to combine. Repeat with the remaining flour, gently folding in the flour in between each addition.

6. Pour the batter into an ungreased 9- or 10-inch tube pan. Smooth out with the back of a spoon.

7. Bake the cake for about 40 minutes, rotating the pan halfway through to ensure even baking. The cake is done when an inserted toothpick comes out clean.

8. Remove the cake from the oven, turn it upside down, and let cool. Run a knife around the outside of the cake to release it from the pan, and serve.

COOKING TIP: Turning the pan upside down while the cake is cooling keeps it from deflating.

Half-Pound Cake

SERVES 4 / PREP TIME: 15 MINUTES / **COOK TIME:** 1 HOUR

Traditionally, pound cake calls for a pound of butter, sugar, and flour—and makes a very large amount! This half-pound recipe yields one loaf. Add some orange or lemon zest for a refreshing spin on the classic buttery flavor.

---

1 cup (2 sticks) unsalted butter

1½ cups white sugar

3 large eggs, at room temperature

1 teaspoon vanilla extract

½ teaspoon kosher salt

2 cups all-purpose flour

½ cup milk

1 teaspoon finely grated orange or lemon zest (optional)

1. Preheat the oven to 350°F. Grease an 8-by-4-inch loaf pan and line with parchment paper.
2. Use the paddle attachment on an electric mixer to cream the butter and sugar until light and fluffy.
3. Add the eggs one a time, scraping down the bowl in between each, until fully incorporated. Add the vanilla and salt.
4. Beat in one-third of the flour, then one-third of the milk, alternating each until everything is combined. Add the zest (if using).
5. Scrape the batter into the prepared loaf pan and bake until a toothpick inserted into the center of the cake comes out clean, for about 1 hour.

CONTINUED >

DIPPERS & SAUCES

6. Remove from the oven and cool in the pan for 10 minutes, then turn the cake out onto a cooling rack. Once cool, remove the parchment paper and serve. Keep covered on the kitchen counter for up to 1 week, or freeze for up to 3 months.

COOKING TIP: Make this recipe with cake flour for an even lighter crumb.

Almond Biscotti

SERVES 6 / PREP TIME: 15 MINUTES, PLUS 20 MINUTES TO COOL / **COOK TIME:** 1 HOUR

These twice-baked Italian cookies are perfect for dunking into everything from specialty coffee and liqueurs to pots of chocolate fondue. This recipe calls for almonds, although you can substitute almost any of your favorite nuts.

---

1 cup raw whole almonds	¾ cup brown sugar
2½ cups all-purpose flour	3 large eggs
1½ teaspoons baking powder	½ cup extra-virgin olive oil
½ teaspoon kosher salt	1 teaspoon vanilla extract
½ cup white sugar	1 tablespoon orange zest (optional)

1. Position a rack in the center of the oven and preheat to 325°F. Line a baking sheet with parchment paper.
2. Put the almonds on the baking sheet and toast for 10 to 12 minutes, or until browned. Allow them to cool, then roughly chop them and set aside.
3. In a medium bowl, whisk together the flour, baking powder, salt, white sugar, and brown sugar. Set aside.
4. In a large bowl, whisk together the eggs, olive oil, vanilla, and orange zest (if using). Add the dry ingredients and mix with a wooden spoon or spatula. Fold in the chopped almonds. The dough will be quite moist.

CONTINUED >

DIPPERS & SAUCES

5. Use a large serving spoon and scoop out the dough onto the prepared baking sheet. Form into 2 even logs about 2 inches wide by 8 inches long. With damp fingers, smooth out the tops.

6. Bake the logs until golden brown and firm to the touch, for about 30 minutes. Then cool them on the sheet for 10 to 15 minutes.

7. Remove the logs from the baking sheet and transfer to a cutting board. Using a serrated knife, slice cookies at a slight angle about ½-inch thick.

8. Return the cookies to the oven for 10 to 15 minutes, turning halfway through. Cool the finished cookies on a cooling rack. Keep covered for up to 1 week on the counter, or 3 months in the freezer.

COOKING TIP: During the second baking, the longer you bake the biscotti, the crispier they will get. If you prefer a slightly softer biscotti, take them out of the oven a little earlier.

Crostini

SERVES 6 / PREP TIME: 5 MINUTES / **COOK TIME:** 8 TO 10 MINUTES

The combination of butter and olive oil in this recipe creates the perfect crispy crostini for dipping into your favorite cheese fondue. Use these crostini for building flavorful canapes and bruschetta for your next party, too.

---

1 day-old baguette

4 tablespoons (½ stick) salted butter, melted

2 tablespoons extra-virgin olive oil

1 garlic clove, minced

1. Preheat the oven to 350°F and line a baking sheet with parchment paper.
2. Cut the baguette crosswise into ¼-inch slices and arrange them on the prepared baking sheet.
3. In a small bowl, mix together the butter, olive oil, and garlic. Brush the butter mixture on top of the baguette. Bake until golden brown and crisp to the touch, for about 9 minutes. Allow to cool completely on the baking sheet and serve.

COOKING TIP: These crostini can be made the day before and stored in an airtight container. If they are a little soft, place the crostini back on the baking sheet and bake for 2 to 3 minutes to make them crispy once more.

Gougères

SERVES 6 / PREP TIME: 10 MINUTES / **COOK TIME:** 35 MINUTES

Gougères are the ultimate in predinner noshing. Be warned: It is impossible to eat only one of these light and airy cheese-studded pastry puffs. Serve as an over-the-top dipper for any cheese fondue.

½ cup water

3 tablespoons unsalted butter

¼ teaspoon kosher salt

¼ teaspoon freshly ground
    black pepper

½ cup all-purpose flour

2 large eggs

2 teaspoons minced chives

¾ cup grated Gruyère
    cheese, divided

1. Preheat the oven to 425°F. Line a baking sheet with parchment paper.
2. In a saucepan, heat the water, butter, salt, and pepper over medium heat until the butter melts.
3. Add all the flour at once and stir vigorously until the mixture pulls away from the sides of the saucepan into a smooth ball. Remove the saucepan from the heat and let it rest for 2 minutes to cool.
4. Transfer the dough to the bowl of a stand mixer fitted with the paddle attachment, or you can use a medium mixing bowl with a handheld mixer.
5. Add the eggs, one at a time, quickly beating the dough with the mixer to make sure the eggs don't cook from the heat of the dough. Once all the eggs have been added, the batter will come together into a smooth mixture.

6. Stir in the chives and ½ cup of Gruyère cheese.
7. Transfer the mixture into a pastry bag fitted with a medium plain tip and pipe the dough into mounds about the size of a small cherry tomato, evenly spaced apart on the prepared baking sheet. Top each puff with the remaining ¼ cup of cheese.
8. Bake for 5 minutes, then turn the oven down to 350°F and bake for 20 to 25 minutes, or until they're completely golden brown. Allow to cool completely on the baking sheet and serve.

COOKING TIP: To ensure your Gougères don't collapse once you remove them from the oven, make a small hole in each with the tip of a sharp knife to allow the steam to escape.

Crisp Gingersnap Cookies

SERVES 6 / PREP TIME: 30 MINUTES, PLUS 40 MINUTES TO CHILL / **COOK TIME:** 15 MINUTES

This recipe yields a buttery, crisp gingersnap cookie that has just the right balance of spices like cloves, cinnamon, ginger, and allspice. Use this cookie as the perfect dipper for Spiked English Custard Fondue (page 103) or any caramel-based dessert fondue.

2⅓ cups all-purpose flour

2 teaspoons ground ginger

½ teaspoon ground allspice

1 teaspoon ground cinnamon

¼ teaspoon ground cloves

2 teaspoons baking soda

¼ teaspoon kosher salt

1 cup (2 sticks) unsalted butter, at room temperature

½ cup brown sugar

1 cup white sugar, divided

1 large egg

⅓ cup molasses

1. Position a rack in the center of the oven and preheat to 350°F. Line 2 baking sheets with parchment paper.
2. In a medium bowl, whisk together the flour, ginger, allspice, cinnamon, cloves, baking soda, and salt.
3. Use an electric mixer with a paddle attachment to cream the butter, brown sugar, and ½ cup of white sugar until it is light and fluffy.
4. Add the egg and beat for about 20 seconds, then scrape down the sides of the bowl; add the molasses and mix well to combine.
5. Add the dry ingredients and mix on low speed until just incorporated. Do not overmix. Refrigerate for 40 minutes.

6. Form the dough into 1-inch balls and roll in the remaining ½ cup of white sugar to coat. Place on the prepared baking sheet about 2 inches apart, then flatten slightly. Bake for 10 to 15 minutes, until completely flat and lightly golden around the edges.

7. Transfer to a cooling rack and allow to cool completely. Store in an airtight container on the counter for up to 1 week, or in the freezer for up to 3 months.

STORE-BOUGHT SHORTCUT: There are some great imported options for gingersnaps. Look for ones from Scandinavia, where these cookies are originally made.

Garlic Bread Knots

SERVES 6 / PREP TIME: 1 HOUR, PLUS 3 HOURS TO RISE / **COOK TIME:** 15 MINUTES

What could be better than dunking homemade garlic bread knots into a pot of bubbling cheese fondue? If you don't have access to a great pizza parlor that will sell you their ready-made pizza dough, these garlic bread knots can be on the table in 20 minutes—and they may disappear just as quickly!

---

1 package active dry yeast (2¼ teaspoons)

1 teaspoon sugar

¾ cup warm water (105°F to 115°F)

2¼ cups all-purpose flour, plus more for dusting

1 teaspoon kosher salt

2 tablespoons extra-virgin olive oil, divided, plus more for coating the bowl

⅓ cup salted butter

1 garlic clove, minced

¼ cup fresh parsley, minced

1. In a small bowl, stir the yeast and sugar together, then add the warm water and let sit for 3 to 5 minutes, or until the mixture starts to foam.
2. In a large bowl, mix together the flour and salt. Make a well in the center and pour in 1 tablespoon of olive oil, then add the yeast mixture. Mix to form a soft dough and knead for 5 to 10 minutes, either by hand or with a mixer fitted with the hook attachment.
3. Place the dough ball in a lightly oiled medium bowl, and cover with plastic wrap. Allow the dough to rest in a draft-free place until the dough doubles in size, for about 90 minutes.
4. Line 2 baking sheets with parchment paper.

5. Put the dough on a floured work surface. Cut into 4 even pieces. Flatten each piece into a 4-by-5-inch rectangle. Use a sharp knife or pizza cutter to slice each rectangle into 8 strips.

6. Roll each piece into a thin rope, then tie it into a knot. Set each knot down on the prepared baking sheet, leaving some space between them so they can rise.

7. Brush each knot with the remaining 1 tablespoon of olive oil and loosely cover with plastic wrap. Let the dough rise again in a draft-free spot until doubled in size, anywhere from 90 minutes to 2 hours.

8. Preheat the oven to 400°F.

9. Uncover the knots and bake for 12 to 15 minutes, or until golden brown. Remove them from the oven and allow them to cool for 5 minutes on a cooling rack.

10. While the bread knots are baking, in a small pot, melt the butter over low heat. Add the garlic and parsley and cook for 1 to 2 minutes. Keep warm.

11. Brush the garlic butter on the bread knots, and serve warm.

STORE-BOUGHT SHORTCUT: Use ready-made pizza dough instead of making your own dough. Jump ahead to step 5 and follow the remaining directions.

MEASUREMENT CONVERSIONS

VOLUME EQUIVALENTS (LIQUID)

US STANDARD	US STANDARD (OUNCES)	METRIC (APPROXIMATE)
2 tablespoons	1 fl. oz.	30 mL
¼ cup	2 fl. oz.	60 mL
½ cup	4 fl. oz.	120 mL
1 cup	8 fl. oz.	240 mL
1½ cups	12 fl. oz.	355 mL
2 cups or 1 pint	16 fl. oz.	475 mL
4 cups or 1 quart	32 fl. oz.	1 L
1 gallon	128 fl. oz.	4 L

VOLUME EQUIVALENTS (DRY)

US STANDARD	METRIC (APPROXIMATE)
⅛ teaspoon	0.5 mL
¼ teaspoon	1 mL
½ teaspoon	2 mL
¾ teaspoon	4 mL
1 teaspoon	5 mL
1 tablespoon	15 mL
¼ cup	59 mL
⅓ cup	79 mL
½ cup	118 mL
⅔ cup	156 mL
¾ cup	177 mL
1 cup	235 mL
2 cups or 1 pint	475 mL
3 cups	700 mL
4 cups or 1 quart	1 L

OVEN TEMPERATURES

FAHRENHEIT	CELSIUS (APPROXIMATE)
250°F	120°C
300°F	150°C
325°F	165°C
350°F	180°C
375°F	190°C
400°F	200°C
425°F	220°C
450°F	230°C

WEIGHT EQUIVALENTS

US STANDARD	METRIC (APPROXIMATE)
½ ounce	15 g
1 ounce	30 g
2 ounces	60 g
4 ounces	115 g
8 ounces	225 g
12 ounces	340 g
16 ounces or 1 pound	455 g

MEASUREMENT CONVERSIONS

INDEX

A

Alcohol, 8. *See also
specific*
Almond Biscotti, 149–150
American cheese, 15
  American Cheeseburger
    Fondue, 44–45
  Hot Queso Fondue,
    34–35
American Cheeseburger
  Fondue, 44–45
Anchovies
  Bagna Cauda Fondue,
    64–65
Angel Food Cake,
  145–146
Appenzeller cheese, 16
Apples
  Caramel Apple–Brie
    Fondue, 101–102
  Steak Sauce, 120–121
Artichoke hearts
  Spinach and Artichoke
    Fondue, 53–54
Asiago cheese, 16
Asian Tempura Fondue,
  66–67
Asparagus
  Grilled Vegetables,
    138–139

B

Bacon
  Baked Brie Fondue, 42
  Canadian Maple-Bacon
    Fondue, 43
  Jalapeño Popper
    Fondue, 57–58
Bagna Cauda Fondue,
  64–65
Baked Brie Fondue, 42
Bananas Foster Fondue,
  115–116
Basil Pesto Fondue,
  38–39
Béarnaise Sauce,
  122–123
Beaufort cheese, 16
  French Fondue, 29
Beef
  American Cheeseburger
    Fondue, 44–45
  Classic Beef Broths,
    135–136
  Italian-Style Oil Fondue,
    70–71
Beer
  Blue Cheese and Leek
    Fondue, 47
  Cheddar and Ale
    Fondue, 46

Hot Queso Fondue,
  34–35
Indian Masala Fondue,
  36–37
Blue Cheese and Leek
  Fondue, 47
Bourbon-Butterscotch
  Fondue, 110
Bourguignonne fondue,
  2–3, 61
  Asian Tempura Fondue,
    66–67
  Bagna Cauda Fondue,
    64–65
  Classic Bourguignonne
    Hot Oil Fondue, 63
  dippers, 62
  German-Style Oil
    Fondue, 72–73
  Greek-Style Oil Fondue,
    74–75
  Italian-Style Oil Fondue,
    70–71
  Spanish-Style Oil
    Fondue, 68–69
Brandy
  French Onion Broth
    Fondue, 89–90
Brie cheese, 16
  Baked Brie Fondue, 42

Caramel Apple–Brie
  Fondue, 101–102
Broccoli
  Steamed Vegetables,
    140–141
Broths. See also Hot pot
  fondue
  Chicken Broth, 137
  Classic Beef Broths,
    135–136
Brussels sprouts
  Steamed Vegetables,
    140–141

C

Cacio e Pepe Fondue, 52
Canadian Maple-Bacon
  Fondue, 43
Caramel Apple–Brie
  Fondue, 101–102
Carrots
  Chicken Broth, 137
  Classic Beef Broths,
    135–136
  Steamed Vegetables,
    140–141
Cauliflower
  Steamed Vegetables,
    140–141
Celery
  Chicken Broth, 137
  Classic Beef Broths,
    135–136

Cheddar and Ale
  Fondue, 46
Cheddar cheese, 17
  American Cheeseburger
    Fondue, 44–45
  Blue Cheese and Leek
    Fondue, 47
  Canadian Maple-Bacon
    Fondue, 43
  Cheddar and Ale
    Fondue, 46
  Indian Masala Fondue,
    36–37
  Pimento Cheese
    Fondue, 48–49
Cheesecake Fondue, 111
Cheese fondue, 2, 23
  American Cheeseburger
    Fondue, 44–45
  Baked Brie Fondue, 42
  Basil Pesto Fondue,
    38–39
  Blue Cheese and Leek
    Fondue, 47
  Cacio e Pepe
    Fondue, 52
  Canadian Maple-Bacon
    Fondue, 43
  Cheddar and Ale
    Fondue, 46
  dippers, 24–25
  Fondue in a Pumpkin,
    50–51

French Fondue, 29
French Onion Fondue,
  40–41
Hot Queso Fondue,
  34–35
Indian Masala Fondue,
  36–37
Italian Fonduta, 30
Jalapeño Popper
  Fondue,
  57–58
Moitié-Moitié
  Fondue, 28
Pimento Cheese
  Fondue, 48–49
Spanish Fondue,
  31–32
Spinach and Artichoke
  Fondue, 53–54
Traditional Swiss
  Fondue, 26–27
Truffle Fondue, 33
Wild Mushroom and
  Herb Fondue,
  55–56
Cheeses. See also
  specific
  quality of, 21
  types of, 15–20
Chicken
  Chicken Broth, 137
  Coq Au Vin Fondue,
    83–84

Chives
  Gougères, 152–153
  Roquefort Dip, 130
Chocolate. *See also* White
  chocolate
  Chocolate Crème
    Fraîche Fondue, 108
  Chocolate-Espresso
    Fondue, 109
  Chocolate Peanut Butter
    Fondue, 107
Cilantro
  Hot Queso Fondue,
    34–35
Classic Beef Broth Hot
  Pot, 79
Classic Beef Broths,
  135–136
Classic Bourguignonne
  Hot Oil Fondue, 63
Classic Chicken Broth Hot
  Pot, 80
Coconut milk/cream
  Peanut Sauce, 124
  Vegan Toasted Coconut
    Fondue, 114
Cognac
  French Onion Broth
    Fondue, 89–90
Comté cheese, 17
  French Fondue, 29
  French Onion Fondue,
    40–41

Coq Au Vin Fondue,
  83–84
Cream cheese
  Cacio e Pepe
    Fondue, 52
  Cheesecake
    Fondue, 111
  Jalapeño Popper
    Fondue, 57–58
  Pimento Cheese
    Fondue, 48–49
  Spinach and Artichoke
    Fondue, 53–54
Crisp Gingersnap
  Cookies, 154–155
Crostini, 151
Cucumbers
  Tzatziki Sauce, 132
Curry Aioli, 128

D

Dessert fondue, 3, 99
  Almond Biscotti,
    149–150
  Angel Food Cake,
    145–146
  Bananas Foster Fondue,
    115–116
  Bourbon-Butterscotch
    Fondue, 110
  Caramel Apple–Brie
    Fondue,
    101–102

Cheesecake
  Fondue, 111
Chocolate Crème
  Fraîche Fondue, 108
Chocolate-Espresso
  Fondue, 109
Chocolate Peanut Butter
  Fondue, 107
Crisp Gingersnap
  Cookies, 154–155
dippers, 100
Half-Pound Cake,
  147–148
Maple Cream
  Fondue, 113
Salted Caramel Fondue,
  105–106
Scottish Shortbread
  Cookies, 143–144
Spiked English
  Custard Fondue,
  103–104
Vegan Toasted Coconut
  Fondue, 114
White Chocolate–
  Marshmallow
  Fondue, 112
Dill
  Tartar Sauce, 125
  Tzatziki Sauce, 132
Dippers, 119
  Almond Biscotti,
    149–150

Angel Food Cake,
145–146
Bourguignonne
fondue, 62
cheese fondue, 24–25
Crisp Gingersnap
Cookies, 154–155
Crostini, 151
dessert fondue, 100
Garlic Bread Knots,
156–157
Gougères, 152–153
Grilled Vegetables,
138–139
Half-Pound Cake,
147–148
hot pot fondue, 78
Scottish Shortbread
Cookies, 143–144
Steamed Vegetables,
140–141

E

Edam cheese, 17
Eggplants
Grilled Vegetables,
138–139
Eggs
Almond Biscotti,
149–150
Angel Food Cake,
145–146
Béarnaise Sauce,
122–123

Crisp Gingersnap
Cookies, 154–155
Gougères, 152–153
Greek Lemon and Garlic
Broth Fondue, 95–96
Half-Pound Cake,
147–148
Italian Fonduta, 30
Italian-Style Oil Fondue,
70–71
Mayonnaise, 126–127
Rouille Sauce, 133
Spanish-Style Oil
Fondue, 68–69
Spiked English Custard
Fondue, 103–104
Tempura Batter, 142
Emmentaler cheese, 17
Traditional Swiss
Fondue, 26–27
Equipment, 12–13
Espresso powder
Chocolate-Espresso
Fondue, 109

F

Fig jam
Baked Brie
Fondue, 42
Fondue
history of, 2
pots, 5–6, 12
styles of, 2–3
tips, 14–15

Fondue in a Pumpkin,
50–51
Fontina cheese, 18
Basil Pesto Fondue,
38–39
Cacio e Pepe
Fondue, 52
Italian Fonduta, 30
Spanish Fondue, 31–32
Truffle Fondue, 33
Wild Mushroom and
Herb Fondue, 55–56
French Fondue, 29
French Onion Broth
Fondue, 89–90
French Onion Fondue,
40–41

G

Garlic Bread Knots,
156–157
German-Style Oil Fondue,
72–73
Ginger
Korean Gochujang
Ketchup, 134
Miso and Lemongrass
Broth, 81–82
Peanut Sauce, 124
Spicy Szechuan Hot Pot,
91–92
Steak Sauce, 120–121
Vietnamese Nuoc Cham
Sauce, 131

Gouda cheese, 18
  Blue Cheese and Leek
    Fondue, 47
  Canadian Maple-Bacon
    Fondue, 43
  Cheddar and Ale
    Fondue, 46
  Indian Masala Fondue,
    36–37
Gougères, 152–153
Greek Lemon and Garlic
  Broth Fondue, 95–96
Greek-Style Oil Fondue,
  74–75
Grilled Vegetables,
  138–139
Gruyère cheese, 18
  Basil Pesto Fondue,
    38–39
  Gougères, 152–153
  Moitié-Moitié
    Fondue, 28
  Traditional Swiss
    Fondue, 26–27
  Wild Mushroom and
    Herb Fondue, 55–56

H

Half-Pound Cake,
  147–148
Havarti cheese, 18
Horseradish Cream, 129

Hot broth fondue. *See*
  Hot pot fondue
Hot oil fondue. *See*
  Bourguignonne fondue
Hot pot fondue, 3, 77
  Classic Beef Broth Hot
    Pot, 79
  Classic Chicken Broth
    Hot Pot, 80
  Coq Au Vin Fondue,
    83–84
  dippers, 78
  French Onion Broth
    Fondue, 89–90
  Greek Lemon and Garlic
    Broth Fondue, 95–96
  Miso and Lemongrass
    Broth, 81–82
  Mushroom Broth
    Fondue, 85–86
  Spicy Mexican Broth
    Fondue, 93–94
  Spicy Szechuan Hot Pot,
    91–92
  Tomato-Saffron Broth
    Fondue, 87–88
Hot Queso Fondue,
  34–35

I

Indian Masala Fondue,
  36–37

Italian Fonduta, 30
Italian-Style Oil Fondue,
  70–71

J

Jalapeño Popper Fondue,
  57–58

K

Kirschwasser, 13, 14
  French Fondue, 29
  Moitié-Moitié Fondue, 28
  Traditional Swiss
    Fondue, 26–27
Korean Gochujang
  Ketchup, 134

L

Leeks
  Blue Cheese and Leek
    Fondue, 47
Lemongrass
  Miso and Lemongrass
    Broth, 81–82
Lemons
  Greek Lemon and Garlic
    Broth Fondue, 95–96
Liqueurs
  Bananas Foster Fondue,
    115–116
  Chocolate-Espresso
    Fondue, 109

M

Manchego cheese
  Spanish Fondue, 31–32
  Spanish-Style Oil
    Fondue, 68–69
Maple Cream
  Fondue, 113
Marshmallows
  White Chocolate–
    Marshmallow
    Fondue, 112
Mascarpone cheese
  Cheesecake
    Fondue, 111
Mayonnaise, 126–127
Meats. *See also specific*
  Asian Tempura Fondue,
    66–67
  Bagna Cauda Fondue,
    64–65
  Classic Beef Broth Hot
    Pot, 79
  Classic Bourguignonne
    Hot Oil Fondue, 63
  Classic Chicken Broth
    Hot Pot, 80
  French Onion Broth
    Fondue, 89–90
  German-Style Oil
    Fondue, 72–73
  Greek Lemon and Garlic
    Broth Fondue, 95–96
  Greek-Style Oil Fondue,
    74–75
  Miso and Lemongrass
    Broth, 81–82
  Mushroom Broth
    Fondue, 85–86
  Spicy Mexican Broth
    Fondue, 93–94
  Spicy Szechuan Hot Pot,
    91–92
Miso and Lemongrass
  Broth, 81–82
Moitié-Moitié
  Fondue, 28
Monterey Jack
  cheese, 19
  Hot Queso Fondue,
    34–35
  Jalapeño Popper
    Fondue, 57–58
  Spinach and Artichoke
    Fondue, 53–54
Mozzarella cheese, 19
  Italian-Style Oil Fondue,
    70–71
  Jalapeño Popper
    Fondue, 57–58
  Spinach and Artichoke
    Fondue, 53–54
Mushroom Broth Fondue,
  85–86
Mushrooms
  Coq Au Vin Fondue,
    83–84
  Grilled Vegetables,
    138–139
  Mushroom Broth
    Fondue, 85–86
  Spicy Szechuan Hot Pot,
    91–92
  Wild Mushroom and
    Herb Fondue, 55–56

N

Nuts
  Almond Biscotti,
    149–150
  Basil Pesto Fondue,
    38–39

O

Oaxaca cheese
  Hot Queso Fondue,
    34–35
Onions
  American Cheeseburger
    Fondue, 44–45
  Chicken Broth, 137
  Classic Beef Broths,
    135–136
  French Onion Broth
    Fondue, 89–90
  French Onion Fondue,
    40–41

Onions (*Continued*)
  Indian Masala Fondue,
    36–37
  Mushroom Broth
    Fondue, 85–86
  Spicy Mexican Broth
    Fondue, 93–94
Oregano
  Greek Lemon and Garlic
    Broth Fondue, 95–96
  Greek-Style Oil Fondue,
    74–75

P

Pantry staples, 6–8
Parmesan cheese
  Basil Pesto Fondue,
    38–39
  Spinach and Artichoke
    Fondue, 53–54
Parsley
  Chicken Broth, 137
  Classic Beef Broths,
    135–136
  Garlic Bread Knots,
    156–157
  Wild Mushroom and
    Herb Fondue, 55–56
Peanut butter
  Chocolate Peanut Butter
    Fondue, 107
  Peanut Sauce, 124
Peanut Sauce, 124

Pecorino Romano cheese
  Cacio e Pepe
    Fondue, 52
Peppers
  Grilled Vegetables,
    138–139
  Hot Queso Fondue,
    34–35
  Jalapeño Popper
    Fondue, 57–58
  Peanut Sauce, 124
  Pimento Cheese
    Fondue, 48–49
  Rouille Sauce, 133
  Spicy Mexican Broth
    Fondue, 93–94
  Vietnamese Nuoc Cham
    Sauce, 131
Pimento Cheese Fondue,
  48–49
Pork. *See also* Bacon;
  Sausage
  Italian-Style Oil Fondue,
    70–71
Potatoes
  Steamed Vegetables,
    140–141
Pots, 5–6, 12
Provolone
  cheese, 19
Pumpkins
  Fondue in a Pumpkin,
    50–51

R

Raclette cheese, 19
  French Onion Fondue,
    40–41
Roquefort Dip, 130
Rosemary
  Wild Mushroom and
    Herb Fondue, 55–56
Rouille Sauce, 133
Rum
  Bananas Foster Fondue,
    115–116

S

Salted Caramel Fondue,
  105–106
Sauces, 119
  Béarnaise Sauce,
    122–123
  Curry Aioli, 128
  Horseradish Cream, 129
  Korean Gochujang
    Ketchup, 134
  Mayonnaise, 126–127
  Peanut Sauce, 124
  Roquefort Dip, 130
  Rouille Sauce, 133
  Steak Sauce, 120–121
  Tartar Sauce, 125
  Tzatziki Sauce, 132
  Vietnamese Nuoc Cham
    Sauce, 131

Sausage
  Hot Queso Fondue,
    34–35
  Spanish Fondue,
    31–32
  Spanish-Style Oil
    Fondue, 68–69
Scottish Shortbread
  Cookies, 143–144
Seafood
  Greek Lemon and Garlic
    Broth Fondue, 95–96
  Miso and Lemongrass
    Broth, 81–82
  Mushroom Broth
    Fondue, 85–86
  Spicy Mexican Broth
    Fondue, 93–94
  Spicy Szechuan Hot Pot,
    91–92
  Tomato-Saffron Broth
    Fondue, 87–88
Spanish Fondue, 31–32
Spanish-Style Oil Fondue,
  68–69
Spicy Mexican Broth
  Fondue, 93–94
Spicy Szechuan Hot Pot,
  91–92
Spiked English Custard
  Fondue, 103–104
Spinach and Artichoke
  Fondue, 53–54

Squash
  Grilled Vegetables,
    138–139
St. Agur cheese, 20
Steak Sauce,
  120–121
Steamed Vegetables,
  140–141
Stilton cheese, 20
Swiss Cheese Union, 2

T

Tallegio cheese, 20
  Truffle Fondue, 33
Tarragon
  Béarnaise Sauce,
    122–123
Tartar Sauce, 125
Tempura Batter, 142
Tequila
  Hot Queso Fondue,
    34–35
Thyme
  Classic Beef Broths,
    135–136
  Coq Au Vin Fondue,
    83–84
  French Onion Broth
    Fondue, 89–90
  French Onion Fondue,
    40–41
  Mushroom Broth
    Fondue, 85–86

Wild Mushroom and
  Herb Fondue, 55–56
Tomatoes
  Hot Queso Fondue,
    34–35
  Steak Sauce, 120–121
Tomato-Saffron Broth
  Fondue, 87–88
Traditional Swiss Fondue,
  26–27
Truffle Fondue, 33
Turkey
  Coq Au Vin Fondue,
    83–84
Tzatziki Sauce, 132

V

Vacherin Fribourgeois
  cheese, 20
  Moitié-Moitié
    Fondue, 28
Vegan Toasted Coconut
  Fondue, 114
Vegetables. See also
  specific
  Grilled Vegetables,
    138–139
  Mushroom Broth
    Fondue, 85–86
  Steamed Vegetables,
    140–141
Vietnamese Nuoc Cham
  Sauce, 131

W

Whiskey
  Spiked English Custard
    Fondue, 103–104
White chocolate
  Cheesecake
    Fondue, 111
  White Chocolate–
    Marshmallow
    Fondue, 112
White Chocolate–
  Marshmallow
  Fondue, 112
Wild Mushroom and Herb
  Fondue, 55–56

Wine, 8
  Baked Brie Fondue, 42
  Cacio e Pepe
    Fondue, 52
  Coq Au Vin Fondue,
    83–84
  French Fondue, 29
  French Onion Broth
    Fondue, 89–90
  French Onion Fondue,
    40–41
  Moitié-Moitié
    Fondue, 28
  Pimento Cheese
    Fondue, 48–49

  Spanish Fondue, 31–32
  Spinach and Artichoke
    Fondue, 53–54
  Traditional Swiss
    Fondue, 26–27
  Truffle Fondue, 33
  Wild Mushroom and
    Herb Fondue, 55–56

Z

Zucchini
  Grilled Vegetables,
    138–139

ACKNOWLEDGMENTS

The African proverb "It takes a village to raise a child" so beautifully sums up my culinary journey. A sincere thank-you to my mentors, teachers, and cheese community who have indulged my many (many!) questions over the years and encouraged me to learn and grow. It is only because of their willingness to share wisdom and expertise that I have been afforded the opportunity to work in an industry that I love. A special thank-you to my dear friend and colleague Kelsie Parsons, who has been my cheerleader from day one.

ABOUT THE AUTHOR

ERIN HARRIS is a chef, cheese specialist (CCP), and food writer who can be found on social media platforms as "the Cheese Poet." Since 2010, Erin has been spreading the word of Canadian-made curd, encouraging her followers to #eatbettercheese, and reminding us why cooking with cheese is the key to living a truly delicious life. Erin has spent time traveling the world as a means to educate her palate and feed her quest for adventure and is always researching her next destination. You can find her leading curated cheese tastings and cooking classes, teaching budding turophiles, and hosting industry cheese nights at her home in Toronto, Canada.